BUSINESS WORLD

Roger Speegle
William B. Giesecke

OXFORD UNIVERSITY PRESS
1983

To Masuko

Oxford University Press

200 Madison Avenue
New York, NY 10016 USA

Walton Street
Oxford OX2 6DP England

OXFORD is a trademark of Oxford University Press.

Library of Congress Cataloging in Publication Data

Speegle, Roger.
  Business world.

  A collection of articles from prominent American
business magazines, adapted for students at a high
intermediate through advanced level of English as a
second language.
    Includes index.
    1. English language—Text-books for foreign speakers.
2. Readers—Business.   3. Business—Addresses, essays,
lectures.   I. Giesecke, William B.   II. Title.
PE1128.S64   1983   428.6'4   82–22345

ISBN 0-19-434109-7 (pbk.)

The following articles were reprinted by permission of the Harvard
Business Review: "Making Pollution Prevention Pay" by Michael
Royston (November/December 1980) Copyright © 1980; "Retail-
ing Without Stores" by Larry J. Rosenberg and Elizabeth C.
Hirschman (July/August 1980) Copyright © 1980; "Social Secu-
rity Hobbles Our Capital Formation" by Martin S. Feldstein (July/
August 1979) Copyright © 1979; " 'Invisible Resource': Women
for Boards" by Felice N. Schwartz (March/April 1980) Copyright
© 1980; "Who Gets Promoted" by Alfred W. Swinyard and Floyd
A. Bond (September/October 1980) Copyright © 1980 by the Pres-
ident and Fellows of Harvard College; all rights reserved.

"It's An Ill Wind: Hazardous Waste Becomes Big Business" (March
16, 1981) reprinted by permission of Barron's National Business
& Financial Weekly, © Dow Jones & Company, Inc. (1981). All
rights reserved.

The following articles were reprinted from Business Week by spe-
cial permission: "Wounded Executives Fight Back on Age Bias"
(July 21, 1980), © 1980; "Earning an Undergraduate Degree at
the Plant" (August 4, 1980), © 1980; "A High-risk Era for the
Utilities (February 23, 1981), © 1981; "Energy Conservation"
(April 6, 1981), © 1981; "Small Business Discovers Its Strength"
(March 10, 1980), © 1980 by McGraw-Hill, Inc., New York, NY
10020. All rights reserved.

"First-Class Secondhand Clothing" adapted from the December
1980 issue of MONEY Magazine by special permission; © 1980,
Time Inc.

"The Free Market Incentive: Self-Interest vs. Greed" reprinted from
the September 1980 issue of Business Economics by permission of
the National Association of Business Economists, © 1980.

The following articles were reprinted by permission of FORTUNE
Magazine: "The Battle for Quality Begins" by Jeremy Main (De-
cember 29, 1980) © 1980 and "Those Business Hunches That Pay"
by Roy Rowan (April 23, 1979) © 1979 Time Inc. All rights re-
served.

Cover Photograph: Colorisic/Penny Tweedie

Printed in the United States of America

To the Student

Business World is a textbook to improve the communicative skills in English of those who have a special interest in the world of business. Based on a variety of authentic articles from prominent American business magazines, the text has as its purpose improvement not only of business reading comprehension and vocabulary, but of oral and listening performance as well. A wide selection of exercises, explanations, model texts, and written and group activities constitute a global approach to the learning of business English.

Fifteen articles have been selected especially for broad, contemporary appeal, from social issues to management problems. The actual language of the articles is unchanged, although most are shortened somewhat. All the more difficult or unusual words— or words with special meanings—are defined in the margins of the text. Exercises based on the business terms in the articles (which have been asterisked *) are designed to assure understanding and to provide students with practice in using them. Grammatical review exercises make use of structures in the articles themselves to improve accuracy of expression. Each

chapter contains a section on the various forms of business communications, such as memos, telexes, letters, summaries, reports both oral and written, and resumés, with clear explanations, many examples, and exercises. Group oral activities are provided which will involve you in realistic communication using structures, terms, phrases, and sentences learned in the chapter, all based on the readings. Finally, there are questions to stimulate you to respond orally or in writing, so that you may apply what you have learned, receiving assurance that you have mastered the elements presented.

Also included, at the end of the book, is an answer key to the Business Vocabulary exercises and Structural Reviews, which will help those students wishing to do independent study. There is also an index of all the words that are glossed, with a reference to the page where each word is defined.

From this wide selection of learning activities, you are sure to find many which are suitable to your special interests in and applications of the English of business.

To the Teacher

A book which is a vehicle for learning must be a usable one, and it is with this fact in mind that this work has been conceived and reconceived. With each reconception, the *variety* of the learning activities, exercises, practices, models, and explanations has been extended and augmented, always keeping in mind the necessity of broad classroom applicability in manifold cultural and educational circumstances. Activities— individual and group, in- and out-of-class, teacher-centered and student-centered—have been balanced and rebalanced to provide the maximum possibilities for creative classroom realization by the teacher, which is after all the primary focus of language learning.

The texts are *authentic* ones from current U.S. periodicals. The articles are shortened, but almost without exception the sentence structure is actually that of the original author. To aid and encourage the reader, for whom reading English is often hard work, business terms and specialized vocabulary are boldfaced and are clearly and simply defined in the margins of the text. Technical distinctions and theoretical issues have been avoided in these definitions in favor of sim-

plicity and clarity. Some definitions take the form of cultural or social notes. Such information, conveniently provided for the student, saves valuable classroom time and obviates expenditure of the teacher's energies in manifold and fragmenting explanations of terms and phrases. Whereas the readings are stimulatingly authentic and sometimes difficult, the notes provide the student with substantial independence.

Following each article are vocabulary exercises stressing business terms or terms that have special business applicability. These are designed to be done either independently by the student or in a classroom context. In using them in our classes, we have also had success in making them into small-group activities. Since most of the words used in the vocabulary exercises have been defined in the margins of the articles, the student should be capable of doing the exercises independently. For your convenience, and your students', all the words appearing in vocabulary exercises are asterisked (*) in the text of the articles. The items used in these exercises have been selected with some special care, and we have included some fairly simple and also some fairly difficult terms in order to provide learning and practice for the wide level of students that are found in most classroom situations. The most important single guideline in the creation of the exercises has been the requirement that they all require *understanding* of the lexical item in question and the sentence in which it is used. The focus of the textbook as a whole is realistic communication.

Grammatical competence is required for any language task, and whereas structure is not uniquely related to the English of business, it cannot be omitted from consideration in the business English teaching task. Students of this textbook are expected to have a sound grammatical background, and the structural explanations and exercises in the Structural Review section are designed as review. Current second or foreign language education theory emphasizes the desirability of highlighting particular grammatical constructions in the context of actual communication events to promote automaticity, and we have incorporated this principle in the work.

The Business Communications section is one of the more immediately applicable sections and has attracted strong interest during test classes. Besides the structure of the language itself, the students need to perceive and appropriate the forms suitable for memos and letters; oral presentations, reports and summaries; conferences; job interviews, resumés, and the like. The discourse forms appropriate to these situations come more easily with explanations and guided practice.

The Action sections in each chapter involve the student in active, creative communication by use of structured debates, panel discussions, interviews, and scenarios for conferences, discussions, and meetings. Indeed, in test class sessions, class spirit generated by the communicative possibilities frequently had to be considerably restricted, and the problem became containing and channeling ideas, not stimulating them. Chiefly responsible for this, we feel, was the appropriateness of the activities for group use and the fact that, in each chapter, *in all the activities up to that point* the ideas, wordings, structures, and discourse features of the readings had been carefully repeated in various forms (vocabulary and grammar exercises and activities, as with business communication tasks). Insofar as possible, each section represents recapitulation of ideas and structures presented in the articles such that realistic use and even automaticity will result.

Finally, the Reaction section, through discussion questions, provides the occasion for student conclusion and even more discussion and debate concerning interpretations and ramifications of the ideas in the articles. We selected the questions for their success in involving test classes in animated—and sometimes opinionated—exchanges. To this end we have purposely included questions which may seem somewhat controversial.

The chapters each form a unified learning experience; the parts of the chapters are structured to reinforce each other, which fact gives teacher and student a healthy sense of accomplishment on its completion. If teachers and students are stimulated by this book to enjoy the richness which we ourselves have found in experimenting with the materials in our own classes, our fondest hopes for the work will be realized.

Acknowledgments

This book's writing reflects the growing need for contextualized English language instruction for non-native speakers of English. Our hope is that it will adequately fulfill at least a part of this need.

The growing number of EFL students requesting contextualized course materials beyond the elementary level are among the first to whom we must acknowledge our gratitude. Without them, the original courses for which this material was developed would not have been possible, and the courses themselves could not have been realized without the kind assistance of Dr. Boyd Collier, Chairman of the Department of Business, St. Edward's University. We also wish to thank Dr. W. L. Hailey, Provost of Texas Wesleyan College, for generously making possible clerical and other support facilitating the preparation of the manuscript.

The book's present form is a vast improvement over its original conception. This is in large part due to the enthusiastic and imaginative assistance of Dr. Marilyn Rosenthal, General Manager of the English Language Teaching Department, Oxford University Press. Also at Oxford, we owe many thanks to Margot Gramer, our editor, who worked so patiently with us on the most tiresome details.

TABLE OF CONTENTS

ENVIRONMENTAL ISSUES

SOCIAL ISSUES

MANAGEMENT

ENVIRONMENTAL ISSUES

CHAPTER ONE: Making Pollution Prevention Pay

By Michael G. Royston

Harvard Business Review

In November 1979, the ministers of the environment from the European countries and representatives from the United States and Canada met in Geneva under the auspices of the Economic Commission for Europe on the Protection of the Environment. Their purpose was to decrease pollution from industrial wastes. The ministers and representatives signed a resolution to "limit, gradually reduce, and prevent" this form of pollution. They also adopted a declaration stating that "economic development and technological progress must be compatible with the protection of the environment" and advocating the use of no-waste technologies in their countries' industries.

Some businesses have long understood that **environmental* protection*** and economic progress can go hand in hand. Consider the following examples:

Ciba-Geigy, the chemical **complex** in Basel, Switzerland, has, with little capital investment, been able to eliminate up to 50% of the pollution from its **operations*** and save an estimated $400,000 a year. By changing its manufacturing **processes*** and **recycling** its water and solvents, it has saved not only money, but also energy.

In the Federal Republic of Germany, Reffelmann Metallverarbeitung KG has recovered its electroplating **liquors** and made a 40% profit on them. ENKA-Glanzstoff AG is increasing* its **marginal profit*** by 30% in recovering zinc from its rayon plant **effluents***.

Minnesota Mining and Manufacturing Company, the **multinational*** based in the United States and known as 3M, has since

Environmental: concerning the surroundings; involving land planning, preservation of public lands and services, control of air and water pollution, and the keeping of coasts and countryside from harm.
Protection: keeping safe, keeping secure.
Environmental protection: the act of keeping lands, air, and water (usually public) safe and free from pollution or other harm.
Complex: industry made up of several branches or parts.
Operations: activities, actions.
Processes: methods, series of actions deliberately undertaken.
Recycling: reusing (of waste products).
Liquors: here, special liquids.
Marginal profit: difference between the cost price and the selling price.
Effluents: wastes from manufacturing processes.
Multinational: company involving more than one country.

Annual: yearly.
Pollutant load: amount of pollution.
Gaseous: in the form of a gas.
Clean-up: any lessening of pollution or polluting agents.

Know-how: practical knowledge, ability to do something.
Potential: possible in the future.
Resources: materials usable in production.

Expending: spending, using up.

Raw materials: goods used in manufacturing a product.
Disposal: throwing away, getting rid of.
Efficiency: effective production with no unnecessary activity or costs.

Managed: directed.
Long-standing: since some time ago.
Installations: systems of machinery arranged for use.

Integrating: using in combination.

Extraction: process of removing or taking out.
Pre-fabricated: constructed beforehand, entirely or in part.

1976 expanded production by 40% and significantly reduced its **annual* pollutant load**. Its liquid effluent has gone from 47 tons to 2.7 tons, its **gaseous*** effluent from 3,000 tons to 2,400 tons, and its solid waste from 6,000 to 1,800 tons. This **clean-up** has resulted in a cost saving of $2,400,000 a year.

By 1976, this company had realized that the cost of meeting increasing demands for pollution control was threatening its profitability. It decided to attack the problem at its root by applying the philosophy that pollutants plus **know-how** equal **potential resources*** and new profits. The company initiated this approach under the slogan "Pollution Prevention Pays" (3P).

In the first nine months of operation in 15 countries, 3P programs eliminated 70,000 tons of air pollutants and 500 million gallons of waste water. Instead of **expending** money, 3M saved $11 million. By viewing pollution as an indicator of waste and an opportunity for profit rather than as a costly threat, the company had, by 1979, saved over $20 million.[1]

New no-waste technologies

The savings possible from such no-waste approaches vary widely from industry to industry and plant to plant. Most of the old technologies and processes in use were selected when the costs of energy, water, and **raw materials** were much lower than they are now and when the costs of waste **disposal** were either very low, or could be ignored. Thus, many existing plants and processes in all industries tend to have a good margin for improving **efficiency***, reducing costs, and minimizing waste and pollution.

Even the best-**managed*** and most efficient businesses are finding opportunities to improve their efficiency, to the benefit of both the economy and the environment. Many of these examples are to be found in Europe because it has a history of high energy and raw material costs as well as **long-standing** environmental concern. Many industrial and municipal **installations** in Europe convert wastes into energy in specially designed incinerators and use waste heat from power plants for district heating.

It was there, in Finland, that the "systems approach" of **integrating** one type of processing plant with another to take care of wastes resulted in combined treatments that are clean, productive, profitable, and capable of generating 50% of their own energy needs.

In the **extraction** and building industries, English Clays has been using its china clay wastes to make **pre-fabricated** houses.

Germany's steel industry has recycled 99% of the water it uses and converted over 90% of its solid wastes into other useful materials.

Some industries are able to turn half their gross pollution load

[1] See Joseph T. Ling, "Developing Conservation Oriented Technology for Industrial Control," in *Non-Waste Technology and Production* (Oxford: Pergamon Press, 1978), p. 313.

Exhibit I
Examples of no-waste technologies

Integrated systems			Wastes avoided
Copper smelting	Sulfuric acid	Fertilizer	Sulfur dioxide, heat, resources
Garbage disposal	Power generation	Drinking water	Land, heat, resources
Garbage disposal	Fuel production	Metal recovery	Land resources
Paper	Alcohol	Protein	Water pollutants
Food preparation	Protein		Water pollutants
Food preparation	Chemicals		Air pollutants, resources
Steel production	Municipal waste water		Water pollutants
Hog production	Cheese		Water pollutants
Electric power	Sulfuric acid		Air pollutants
Domestic water	Industrial water	Pollutant recovery	Water pollutants, resources
Whiskey production	Animal feed		Water pollutants, resources
Timber	Plywood	Pulp	Water pollutants, resources
Heat	Power generation		Air pollutants, heat, resources
Metallurgy	Paper		Air pollutants, heat, resources
Aluminum	Cryolite		Air pollutants, energy, resources
Alloy steel tubes	Pigments		Water pollutants
Titanium dioxide	Pigments	Magnetic tape	Water pollutants
Steel production	Ceramics		Solid wastes
Phosphates	Plasterboard		Water pollutants
Mining	Building materials (bricks, cement, aggregate)		Solid wastes
Electric power	Insulating bricks		Solid wastes
China clay	Prefabricated houses		Solid wastes
Mining	Recreation		Land
Electric power	Heating for homes, fishponds, fields		Heat
Animal waste	Gas		Water pollutants

to profit before having to pay for the hard task of cleanup, and many of them are in North America.

Hylsa, the steel company in Mexico, is using the sponge iron process to **implement** direct **reduction** technology and prevent the massive pollution of coke ovens, which cost U.S. Steel over $600 million to clean up recently at its Clairton works.

Shell Oil in Canada has been disposing of its **refinery sludge*** by **ploughing** it into the prairie and increasing **barley** yields from 18% to 31%.

In the United States, the paper companies have begun to look at their industrial wastes as ways of making money.[2]

To implement: to put into effect or operation.
Reduction: here, involving purification by removal of oxygen.

Refinery sludge: very thick liquid waste from processing crude oil.
Ploughing: working or turning up soil, as in farming.
Barley: a kind of grain.

[2] United Nations, "Money from Wastes," *Development Forum*, January–February 1977, p. 3.

By-product: anything produced as a result of making something else.
Potent: here, strong.
Stationed: placed in position.

As a **by-product*** of processing at its Bellingham, Washington, plant, Georgia Pacific is producing 190-proof alcohol "so pure and **potent**" that the Treasury Department has **stationed** men in the plant full-time to make sure that none of it is converted to drinking liquor before its sale to industrial users.

Organizing for profit

Exploit: take advantage of, profit from.
Prevention: keeping something undesirable from happening.
Corporatewide: throughout the entire corporation.
Innovation: any new process or device.
Delegating: here, giving.
Shop floor: where the work of a factory or plant is actually taking place.
Comprising: including.
Audit: check or verify financially.

How can companies best **exploit** their own pollution **prevention*** opportunities: The key to 3M's success has been giving **corporatewide** recognition to the importance of technological **innovation*** in making the company efficient and profitable, **delegating** responsibility and initiative to the **shop floor** and rewarding all company personnel who get involved in 3P programs.

Each 3M factory has its own plant energy and environment committee **comprising** the plant engineer as chairman, the maintenance supervisor, the control engineer, the manufacturing supervisor, the division engineer, and an industrial engineer. Their job is to set targets for waste avoidance, establish programs with shop floor personnel, report progress to management, **audit** savings, and report to the central committee.

Mobilized: collected or assembled together for service or use.
Abatement: lessening or decreasing.
Proposal: formal suggestion.
Monetary: financial.
Deferred: put off, left until later.
Running costs: costs of day-to-day operation.

At 3M all corporate personnel from the shop floor upward are **mobilized*** to contribute their knowledge and observations to the pollution **abatement** programs adopted. To qualify as a 3P program, a **proposal*** has to eliminate or reduce a pollutant; bring about reduced energy use or more efficient use of raw materials like water; include some innovative features; and bring **monetary** benefit through reduced or **deferred** controls or manufacturing costs, increased sales of existing or new products, or reduced capital or **running costs**. Pollution has been efficiently lessened, not by installing pollution control plants, but by reformulating products, redesigning equipment, modifying processes, or recovering materials for reuse.

Growth *boost*

Boost: here, improvement.

If taking such a positive approach to environmental protection can help companies maintain their profit, it can also help them grow. In the United States this year, environmental business has been almost a $50 billion affair and has recently been increasing 20% a year.

Subsidiaries: companies with more than 50% of the stock owned by another company.
Turnover: amount of business done.

This new commercial area has brought in its wake a wave of new businesses. In the Federal Republic of Germany, more than 200 new companies have recently been set up to provide environmental products and services. In the United States, there are companies like Apollo Chemical Co., which started in the air pollution business some 15 years ago employing 10 people, but which now employs over 400 and has **subsidiaries** around the world. Another is Waste Management, Inc., a garbage-handling business based on a new technology that yields a **turnover** of $350 million.

Even more significant, many large companies have added divi-

Exhibit II
Number of innovations in which environmental concerns have been considered

Industry	France	Federal Republic of Germany	Japan	Netherlands	United Kingdom	Total
Automobiles	4	12	2		10	28
Chemicals	9	12	6	5	12	44
Computers	5	9	7		10	31
Consumer electronics	7	8	6	3	8	32
Textiles	10	6		7	6	29
Total	35	47	21	15	46	164

Source: National Support for Science and Technology: An Examination of Foreign Experience (Cambridge: Massachusetts Institute of Technology, 1976)

sions to provide environmental goods and services. In the United States, Boeing, FMC, Exxon, Dow Chemicals, 3M, and Caterpillar Tractor all market environmental products and services. In Europe, Shell, BP, Ciba-Geigy, Krupp, and Philips market specialized environmental services.

New growth areas tend to stem from technological innovation, and innovation tends to result from external need or pressure. Environmental pressure generates innovation.

Environmentally **induced** economic activity continues to stimulate the economy. It is an estimated 2% of the gross national product in countries like the United States. The amount of employment **engendered** by all aspects of environmental protection in the United States was, at the 1977 Environmental Improvement Council Conference, reported to be 2 million jobs. Direct employment induced by the National Environmental Policy Act runs at about 75,000.[3]

Induced: caused, brought about.
Engendered: created.

Japan, in recession in 1974, used strict pollution control to boost construction and engineering and hence restimulate the economy; 20% of its economic growth since then can be attributed to its new strict environmental legislation.[4] Japanese companies are world leaders in supplying some kinds of advanced pollution control equipment.

Survival of the fittest

In determining the direction of their future growth, companies as well as nations will more and more have to take environmental concerns into account. The ultimate objective of the corporation is survival, and reaching that depends very much on the adaptation of the corporation to its environment.

Such major companies as Shell and BP are directing their development by **forecasting** from **scenarios***. They describe all the

Forecasting: predicting, foretelling.
Scenarios: possible series of events or story outlines usually to make a specific point or for a specific purpose.

[3] *Eighth Annual Report of the Council on Environmental Quality* (Washington, D.C.: U.S. Government Printing Office, 1977), p. 332.
[4] Organization for Economic Cooperation and Development, "Prevention Less Costly than Cure," *OECD Observer*, May 1979, p. 9.

Services: in business, something done to benefit others for pay.

possible environmental conditions that might control their growth and make decisions accordingly. AKZO, the Dutch chemical multinational, constructs elaborate scenarios based on the social, political, physical, economic, and technological environments that it feels may prevail in the future and then determines which products and **services*** will be most compatible with such conditions.

Impact: result, effect.

More and more companies are assessing the environmental **impact** of projects they are about to introduce. Enterprises accept the validity of environmental concern and encourage environmental awareness on their staffs. They can minimize the negative and maximize the positive impacts of their new projects.

Press: here, publicity.

They can also prevent their projects from being blocked by the courts or by citizen protest actions. By becoming concerned about environmental impact ahead of time, companies can avoid costly delay, bad **press**, and heavy financial burden.

Payoff: the long-awaited reward.

The *payoff*

Ecological: having to do with living things and their relationship to the environment.

If a company looks at economic questions in an **ecological** way and at ecological questions in an economic way, it can make pollution prevention pay in relation to three corporate objectives. By focusing attention on waste avoidance and efficient operation, it can increase profit. By investigating new areas in which to develop products and services, it can grow. By avoiding conflict over new projects and winning acceptance for them by looking at them with an eye to the new environmental values, it can improve its chances of surviving.

1. Business Vocabulary

A. Complete the sentences with the appropriate form of the word in parenthesis.

   1. (environment)   Many businesses are making their _____ concerns profitable.
   2. (process)   Chemical companies are now beginning to change their manufacturing_____ .
   3. (gas)   Many pollutants are in _____form.
   4. (resource)   Pollutants are now seen as possible _____ .
   5. (prevent)   Companies are concerned with the _____ of pollution.
   6. (innovate)   Many businesses such as 3M are recognizing the importance of promoting technological _____ .
   7. (operate)   Large _____ are finding profitable methods of using waste materials.
   8. (mobile)   The 3M Corporation has _____ all personnel in its efforts to prevent pollution.
   9. (propose)   _____ for eliminating or reducing a pollutant are being sought at some companies.
  10. (protect)   Currently, many companies are concerned with environmental _____ .
  11. (efficient)   Businesses are concerned with the _____ of their operation while reducing pollution.

B. Below is a brief summary of the article. From the list of words, there is one choice that is most suitable for each blank in the article. Each word is used one time. Be sure to use the appropriate form.

marginal profit	refinery sludge
services	by-product
managed	effluents
multinational	annual
scenario	increase

   This article looks at how businesses are working toward environmental protection at the same time as making economic progress. For example, the 3M Company, a _____ based in the U.S., has significantly reduced its _____ pollutant load. Another company, Georgia-Pacific, is producing salable alcohol as a _____ of its normal processing. Shell Oil of Canada has found that some material such as _____ may be used to _____ agricultural production. Elaborate _____ are used by AKZO in planning future products and _____ . Not only are poorly _____ businesses finding opportunities to improve their efficiency: a significant amount of _____ can be gained by recovering usable material from _____ .

2. Structural Review

A. Expressing manner and purpose with *by* and *to*:

Some kinds of verb phrases (for example, PREP + VB + *-ing* or *to* + INF) are used very freely in technical and business writing. In the course of his article, the author uses *by* with a verb telling *how* a dozen times. The full form of this use *by* is *by means of*. It indicates that the verb following *by* tells *how*. A verb following *by* ends in *-ing*.

> Example 1: Ciba-Geigy has saved not only money but also energy *by changing* its manufacturing processes.

> Example 2: By 1979, 3M has saved over $20 million *by viewing* pollution as an opportunity for profit.

Almost as often, the author uses *to* before a verb to tell *why*. A verb after *to* has the infinitive form.

> Example 1: Many large companies have added divisions *to provide* environmental goods and services.

> Example 2: *To boost* construction and engineering in a recession period, Japan used strict pollution control legislation.

Using either *by* or *to*, combine the following pairs of sentences into one, changing the verb if necessary.

> Example: Shell Oil in Canada has been disposing of its refinery waste. It is ploughing it into the prairie.

> Solution: Shell Oil in Canada has been disposing of its refinery waste *by ploughing* it into the prairie.

1. English Clays has been using its china clay wastes. It is making pre-fabricated houses.
2. The Treasury Department has stationed men in the plant. They are making sure that no alcohol is converted to drinking liquor.
3. Such major companies as Shell and BP are directing their own development. They are forecasting from scenarios.
4. Hylsa of Mexico is using the sponge iron process. It is implementing direct reduction technology and preventing massive pollution of its coke furnaces.
5. Companies can avoid costly delay. They become concerned about environmental impact ahead of time.
6. A company can increase profits. It focuses attention on waste avoidance.
7. At 3M all corporate personnel from the shop floor upward are mobilized. They are contributing their knowledge and observations.
8. Plants have efficiently lessened pollution. They have recovered materials for reuse.
9. In Germany more than 200 new companies have set themselves up. They are providing environmental products and services.

10. The corporation is surviving. It is adapting to its environment.
11. ENKA-Glanzstoff AG is increasing its marginal profit. It is recovering zinc from its rayon plant effluents.
12. By 1976, 3M had decided to attack the problem at its roots. It applied its know-how.
13. The company is increasing profits. It is focusing attention on waste avoidance.
14. Some companies are turning waste to profit. They are taking a positive view of pollution.
15. A company can grow. It investigates new areas in which to develop products and services.
16. The technology of an industry must have a good margin for improving efficiency. It economizes by means of a no-waste approach.

B. Communicating other meanings with prepositions and verbs plus *-ing*

In the article there are also other prepositions which go before verbs ending in *-ing*. Most verbs following prepositions must end in *-ing*.

> Example: The industry changed to a new process *without giving* consideration to future environmental demands.

In this article, there are four such prepositions used: *for*, *of*, *in*, and *instead of*. Choose the best of these four prepositions to complete the blanks in the following sentences:

1. (   ) expending money, 3M saved $11 million by viewing pollution as an indicator of waste.
2. As a by-product (   ) processing at its Washington plant, Georgia Pacific is producing 190-proof alcohol.
3. ENKA-Glanzstoff AG is increasing its marginal profit by 30% (   ) recovering zinc from its rayon plant effluents.
4. The key to 3M's success has been giving corporatewide recognition to the importance of technological innovation (   ) making the company efficient and profitable.
5. In the United States, the paper companies have begun to look at their industrial wastes as ways (   ) making money.
6. Many existing plants and processes in all industries tend to have a good margin (   ) improving efficiency.

3. Business Communications

Summarization

The ability to *summarize* is a skill vital to both oral and written business transactions. A summary presents only the most important information in a concise form. You will need this skill when writing business reports or in presenting lengthy oral explanations.

The following questions are based on the text. Answer each question with one complete sentence.

> Example: *Question*: Some businesses have long understood that economic progress can go hand in hand with what?
>
> *Solution*: Economic progress can go hand in hand with environmental protection.

1. The three examples of companies cited in the introduction show the reader what?
2. What sort of technologies can be found in many industries and what does this mean for attempts to reduce pollution?
3. Not only poorly managed businesses but also what other kinds of businesses in Europe and North America are capable of benefiting the economy and the environment?
4. As an example of how a company works toward pollution prevention, how did 3M organize in its effort to reduce or lessen pollution?
5. Besides helping companies maintain or increase profits, what has been another benefit of the concern with pollution?
6. How does this new business help a nation's economy?
7. How are some companies planning for the future?
8. How can companies make pollution prevention pay?

Taking the answers to the questions in the above exercise and putting them together, we have a paragraph similar to the one that follows. Compare your paragraph to the one below. Note that this paragraph is a *summary* of the most important information found in the article.

Example summary

Economic progress can go hand in hand with environmental protection. The examples given demonstrate that pollution may be greatly lessened while making a profit from recycling wastes. Many industries use old technologies and processes and thus have a good margin for improving efficiency and minimizing waste and pollution. Also, well-managed and efficient businesses in Europe and North America are capable of improving efficiency to the benefit of both the economy and the environment. The 3M Corporation recognized the importance of technological innovation, delegated responsibility and initiative to the shop floor and rewarded personnel for getting involved in its pollution program. A new commercial area has been created—the environmental business. Environmentally induced economic activity stimulates the economy by creating new technological innovations and by employing more people. Some companies plan by forecasting from scenarios based on the possible social, political, economic, and technological environmental conditions that may exist in the future. If a company looks at economic questions in an ecological way and at ecological questions in an economic way, it can make pollution prevention pay.

4. Action

Informal class debate

Divide the class into two teams to debate informally the issue of pollution:

Team A: Developing countries should for the most part disregard pollution problems, since economic problems are so very important to the well-being of their peoples.

Team B: Every nation has equal moral responsibility to work in every possible way against the dangers of pollution, which are a world-wide problem and do not belong to any one nation.

Allow each team five to seven minutes of group preparation followed by a three-minute presentation (timed with a watch). Allow time for a rebuttal of three minutes by each team.

5. Reaction

Questions for Discussion

Divide into groups and discuss one or more of the following questions. Report your group's response to the whole class.

1. Many of the businesses cited in this article are in Europe and the United States where laws and economic conditions have forced industries to create the new, no-waste technologies. Do you think that industries in other nations, where laws and economic conditions are different, will be willing to make the extra effort necessary for controlling pollution and waste?

2. The article states that "most of the old technologies and processes in use were selected when costs of energy, water and raw materials were much lower than they are now." New, no-waste technologies will probably be more expensive than the old ones. Will businesses in energy-rich nations be willing to spend the extra money for this new technology?

3. This article focuses upon businesses which have been able to make a profit from pollution clean-up. This, of course, is consistent with a basic fact of business: the profit motive. What about businesses which cannot make a profit on waste clean-up? Will they be willing to spend money on cleaning up or preventing pollution when they cannot make a profit by doing so?

4. The need for environmental protection has created more than 200 new companies in Germany alone. In the U.S., environmental divisions of large companies continue to employ more and more people. Clearly, environmentally related business benefits the economy. Will this sort of business be of interest to businessmen in the developing nations? Where will business in the developing nations be most concerned with investing its money? Do you foresee environmental businesses becoming an important part of the economy of developing nations?

CHAPTER TWO: It's an Ill Wind: Disposal of Hazardous Waste Becomes Big Business

Roscoe C. Born   *Barron's*

Ill: sick; evil.
Hazardous: dangerous.

Pesticide/herbicide: two kinds of poison, "-cide" means to kill; a "pest" is any small, undesirable animal; "herb" indicates plant life.
Infamous: well-known for something bad.
Agent Orange: a herbicide infamous because of both its questionable use by the U.S. military in Viet Nam and its aftereffects on those exposed to it.
To dispose of: to get rid of in a desired manner.

Environmental Protection Agency (EPA): an arm of the U.S. federal government which has the responsibility of administering laws and rules to preserve the environment.
Vacated: left.

Generators: companies which create or produce waste.
Handlers: those who deal with or manage or control materials.
Liable: responsible.
Risks: dangers, hazards.

Consider the case of Hercules, Inc., which in 1961 bought a one-time **pesticide** plant in Arkansas and began manufacturing **herbicides,** including the now **infamous Agent Orange** (chief customer: the U.S. military). Hercules tried—ineffectively—to **dispose of*** wastes it inherited at the site as well as its own waste products. In 1971 Hercules leased, then sold, the site to another herbicide maker*, now known as Vertac Chemical Corp., and has had nothing to do with the place since.

Yet in 1980, on complaint of the State of Arkansas and the U.S. **Environmental Protection Agency (EPA),** a Federal court ordered Vertac to undertake costly environmental clean-up in the area— with Hercules to share the cost. All of this despite the court's finding that both Hercules and Vertac had cooperated with environmental agencies, and despite the fact that the laws that caught them in 1980 didn't even exist when Hercules **vacated** the site in 1971.

The Hercules case is only one of dozens, perhaps soon to be thousands, in which **generators*** or **handlers** of waste material are finding themselves **liable,** for health and environmental **risks,** past, present and future. Douglas MacMillan, director of EPA's Hazardous Waste Enforcement Task Force, estimates that "so far we have either completed, underway, or legally committed some $51.5 million in privately financed site clean-up." And that is only the beginning.

What could Hercules and Vertac have done to protect them-

Note: The title of the article is taken from a proverb, "It's an ill wind that blows nobody good," which is usually interpreted to mean, "Even if things are very bad, there's something good in it for someone." In this case, the point is that getting rid of dangerous waste products has become very profitable for some companies.

selves against costly after-the-fact remedies? Perhaps little more than they did or knew how to do then, judging from court documents. But a present-day generator of hazardous waste has an **out*** now. For one thing, he can **turn** his waste **over*** to a government-approved handler and be forever **off the hook***, under regulations promulgated by the EPA in compliance with a **key** law: The Resource Conservation and Recovery Act (commonly known as RCRA, or Ricra).

Out: here, solution, answer, or escape from a difficult situation.
Turn over: to give over control.
Off the hook: no longer responsible.
Key: very important, vital.

With RCRA, passed in 1976 but only now about to be fully implemented, comes a **bonanza*** for an industry already growing, now seemingly on the threshold of **booming** expansion. This is the industry that can get the generators of hazardous waste off the hook, by taking over, transporting, **treating***, storing or disposing of their harmful by-products. For **handsome*** fees, of course. All of this is to be done under the computerized eye of the Environmental Protection Agency, in cooperation with the states. The tougher EPA and similar state agencies get, the better business will be for professional handlers of hazardous waste.

Bonanza: great wealth or riches.
Booming: increasing with surprising strength (usually financially), increasing suddenly.
Treating: dealing with, giving care to, putting through a process.
Handsome: good-looking; here, large.

Nor is there any **dearth*** of material to handle. The EPA estimates that "some 50 million metric tons of possibly hazardous wastes are produced annually in the United States," and that amount is expected to grow by 3.5% annually.

Dearth: lack.

A booming decade?

The future appears to be generally bright for the professional waste-handling industry, or parts of it. An EPA official familiar with RCRA and the new regulations confides, "I think this is really going to be a booming business over the next 10 years."

According to a study done for EPA by Booz, Allen & Hamilton and Putnam, Hayes & Bartlett: "The hazardous-waste management industry has experienced rapid growth since its **inception*** in the 1960s." In the 1971–80 period, the study says, "**revenues** grew at a rate of approximately 20% per year."

Inception: beginning, start.
Revenues: income, receipts of money.

Richard L. Hanneman, director* of government affairs for the National Solid Wastes Management Association, says membership hasn't grown much since the creation of strict environmental laws, but **legislation** "has produced a growth in revenues and strength of our member companies. They have **prospered** and will prosper far more as RCRA proceeds."

Legislation: the making of laws.
Prospered: was successful (with money).

What **transformed*** an ordinary trash business into a **thriving***, modern industry, starting in the Sixties, was the growth of public sentiment demanding more protection for public health and environment. Congress responded by passing a number of environmental laws, most important the Solid Waste Act of 1965. Further **amendments ensued** until finally the Resource Conservation and Recovery Act of 1976 ordered strict controls of more unusual substances, classified as hazardous wastes. (Superfund, the $1.6 billion waste clean-up legislation, was not to come until late 1980.)

Transformed: changed completely.
Thriving: growing, flourishing.
Amendments: formal changes.
Ensued: happened later or as a result.

Missed deadline

RCRA directed the EPA to issue **regulations** identifying what substances are hazardous and **tracking** those substances from their creation to their disposal. EPA found the **task*** was complex almost beyond comprehension; its slow progress toward understanding the size of the problem and how to **deal with*** it caused EPA to miss, by far, the 18-month deadline Congress set for issuing the RCRA regulations.

Finally, last November, the bulk of RCRA regulations were in place, and **drastically** different methods of handling hazardous waste began to take shape.

Essentially, the system works in this way: EPA has classified some 200 substances as hazardous and is ready to add more if necessary. Waste generators can **consult** this list to determine if they are creating hazardous waste, or they can declare their wastes hazardous on their own if they believe them to be so. Every generator, transporter, treater, storer or disposer of these wastes must notify EPA of the fact and get an EPA identification number, which must be used in any hazardous waste **transaction**. All of them report to EPA annually on how much waste they handled and how they handled it.

Next step: Getting EPA permits to continue or begin operation. Generators don't need permits, unless they operate their own treatment, storage or disposal **facilities**. Neither do **transporters***. But every company that does treat, store or dispose of hazardous waste must meet standards **set down*** by EPA and get an EPA permit.

In RCRA's creation-disposal **concept**, a generator of hazardous waste that wants to be rid of the problem prepares a waste shipment (again, according to EPA standards), attaches a **manifest** identifying the material and stating its destination, arranges with an approved receiving facility and turns the shipment over to a transporter. When the generator gets back his copy of the manifest proving that the shipment did arrive at the destination, he's **in the clear***. If he hears nothing from the receiving facility, he must first try to find out what went wrong, then notify EPA if he can't **track down*** the shipment. The newly formed Hazardous Waste Enforcement Task Force in EPA stands ready to seek fines and criminal penalties for **violators***. A facility can also lose its license if it violates EPA standards—and thus be cut out of business.

Enter Superfund

As if this were not enough to swell the **coffers*** of professional waste-handling companies, there's Superfund—a $1.6 billion **kitty***, established in the closing days of Congress in December of 1980, for emergency environmental clean-ups. (Tax money makes up $220 million of the fund; the rest comes from the chemical industry.) Superfund differs from RCRA in that RCRA attempts to control **disposition** of hazardous waste from now on. Superfund permits

Regulations: governmental rules.
Tracking: observing or watching something constantly as it moves or changes.
Task: something that must be done, job.
To deal with: to take care of, handle, take action on.

Drastically: radically, extremely, seriously.

Consult: go to for information or advice.
Transaction: business deal; here, involving movement from place to place.

Facilities: plants or equipment.
Transporters: those who carry something; specifically, those who have the responsibility of carrying away waste.
Set down: established, imposed.

Concept: idea.
Manifest: a list of freight or cargo.
In the clear: no longer in danger.
Track down: trace to its origins, search until found.
Violators: those who act without regard to something, as against the law.

Coffers: money boxes.
Kitty: any joint or cooperative pool or fund of money.
Disposition: the act of moving or clearing away.

WIDE WORLD PHOTOS

the government to move quickly to clean up dangerous wastes (such as Love Canal[1]) immediately, no matter when the waste was **dumped**, without first hunting down the **culprit***. After Superfund money has dealt with the emergency, the **parties*** responsible may be found and held liable (sometimes for triple damages), thus further discouraging waste generators from trying to bury their wastes secretly, outside the creation-to-disposal system.

So all looks fine for the future of the hazardous-waste handlers, right? Not **altogether**.

One problem is the uncertainty for most regulatory agencies—including EPA—that began with Ronald Reagan's administration. No. 1, Reagan's people don't like excessive regulation. No. 2, they don't like big federal budgets to run the bureaucracy. There's talk in Washington that President Reagan would like to turn over many EPA **functions** to the states, to enforce under general federal **guidelines**.

Dumped: thrown away.
Culprit: guilty one.
Parties: persons responsible for an action or activity, often a legal term; actor.

Altogether: completely.

Functions: operations.
Guidelines: statements describing acceptable activity.

[1]Love Canal, in New York State, was the site of a hazardous waste scandal where dangerous chemicals were dumped and later affected the health of the population.

Capacity: ability to deal with demands.
Over: the prefix "over-" generally means "too much."
Surplus: more than enough, too much.

To bar: to stop, to prevent.
Weighing: considering, evaluating.
County: division of a state.
Sales campaign: publicity program.

Capital-intensive: requiring a great deal of money to begin (a business activity).
Trend: pattern or new pattern.
Gobbling up: swallowing whole.

On-site: at one's own location (in this case, the generator's).
To detoxify: to remove the poison from.
Benign: not dangerous, harmless.

Entail: involve, have as a necessary result.
Inelastic: unchangeable.

Millennium: a thousand years.

Another potential problem is the industry's **capacity**—finding enough sites to dispose of the rising mountains of hazardous waste. Because the industry **over**built in the middle Seventies, expecting earlier action on RCRA, there's actually a **surplus** of capacity for the immediate future.

But beyond the next year or two, new sites will have to be found for disposal facilities, and that's a problem the industry is not certain it can overcome. "It's very, very severe," concedes Hanneman. No community wants a hazardous-waste dump located nearby, and many states try to **bar*** interstate shipments. While a community will live with a dump site for its own waste, nobody wants to become a dumping ground for other communities or other states. Colorado is **weighing*** legislation to let each **county** decide itself. Environmental groups, the industry, and the government admit it will take a tremendous **sales campaign** to overcome public opposition, to convince the public that properly managed facilities offer no health threat.

"In addition to stopping many attempts at creating new facilities," says the Booz, Allen study, "intense public opposition has slowed expansion of existing facilities and, in several instances, brought about the closing of some operating facilities."

The high cost of sophisticated new disposal facilities is another concern of the industry. So **capital-intensive** is the business that, according to an EPA study, only the largest firms may be able to survive. The **trend** toward industry concentration may accelerate—the big **gobbling up** the small.

High cost and the difficulty in expanding or finding new sites, in fact, may eventually cause another shift in the industry: a trend to **on-site** facilities, using newer technologies to **detoxify** wastes or change them into **benign** or even useful materials.

In a recent study, the General Accounting Office, the investigative arm of Congress, found that "for the long-term interests of the country," land disposal should be drastically reduced because "eventually we will run out of land on which to develop sites." Yet it's the least expensive and most commonly used method today.

For all of that, the Booz, Allen study for the EPA concludes: "Although handling hazardous waste may **entail** risks and significant capital investment, the profitability outlook for the industry is generally favorable. Potentially high profits are possible because the demand for hazardous-waste management services is relatively **inelastic** while the supply of additional capacity may be scarce."

Or, as Lisa Friedman, in EPA's office of the general counsel, puts it: "We are going to continue to generate hazardous waste over the next **millennium**. We've got to go some place with it. Somebody's got to manage it."

1. Business Vocabulary

A. Circle the letter next to the word or words most similar in meaning to the italicized term in the sentence.

1. Since 1980, generators of hazardous waste have had an *out*.
    a. possible solution   b. a job   c. a fee

2. One thing waste generators can do is *turn* their wastes *over* to the government.
    a. turn upside down   b. give, deliver
    c. investigate, study

3. When wastes are turned over to the government, the generator is forever *off the hook*.
    a. uninterested   b. not responsible, not liable
    c. improving, increasing

4. The RCRA regulations are a *bonanza* for the waste disposal industry.
    a. a boom in business   b. a hindrance
    c. an incentive

5. The waste disposal companies receive a *handsome* fee for their work.
    a. fair, reasonable   b. standard   c. good, large

6. There is no *dearth* of wastes to be disposed of.
    a. lack   b. abundance   c. increase

7. The hazardous waste management industry has been booming since its *inception* in the 1960s.
    a. difficult period   b. expansion   c. beginning

8. Ordinary trash businesses were *transformed* into *thriving* industries.
    a. created   a. working
    b. discovered   b. successful, growing
    c. changed   c. declining

9. EPA's *task* is a complex one.
    a. desire, want   b. job, duty   c. effort

10. EPA finds the complex problems very difficult to *deal with*.
    a. accept   b. handle   c. understand

11. Companies that treat, store, or dispose of hazardous wastes must meet standards *set down* by EPA.
    a. created, established, designed   b. approved
    c. recognized

12. When a waste generator receives the manifest from the waste's final destination, he is *in the clear*.
    a. legally bound   b. licensed
    c. no longer responsible

13. If the waste generator cannot *track down* the waste, he must notify EPA.
    a. buy and pay for   b. hunt and find
    c. see and recognize

14. RCRA is going to swell the *coffers* of professional waste handlers.
    a. work load   b. expenses   c. money boxes

15. The Superfund is a $1.6 billion *kitty* established by Congress.
    a. fund   b. bank   c. revenue

16. RCRA attempts to control *disposition* of hazardous wastes.
    a. creation   b. purchase   c. getting rid
17. Superfund is not concerned with the *culprit* but with cleaning up dangerous wastes.
    a. guilty person   b. damage   c. hazard
18. Superfund finds the responsible *parties* after cleaning up the waste.
    a. behaviors   b. persons, companies   c. systems
19. Many states try to *bar* interstate shipments of hazardous wastes.
    a. control   b. certify   c. make illegal
20. Colorado is *weighing* legislation that would let each county decide for itself about waste dump sites.
    a. creating   b. considering   c. stopping

B.   Noun Agents

$$VB + \text{-}er = \text{noun agent}$$

$$VB + \text{-}or = \text{noun agent}$$

Nouns that perform an action or task are sometimes called *noun agents*. They may represent either people or things. Many of them in this chapter represent people or groups of people such as companies and are formed by adding *-er* to some verbs and *-or* to other verbs. If the verb ends in *-e*, that *-e* must be dropped before adding the ending.

For example, the following verbs require the addition of *-or* for the creation of the noun agent form:

VERB	NOUN AGENT	
direct	director	(Notice the *-e* of
operate	operator	*operate* must be
generate	generator	eliminated.)
violate	violator	

But other verbs require *-er* to create the noun agent form:

VERB	NOUN AGENT
transport	transporter
store	storer
make	maker
dispose	disposer

Complete the following sentences with the noun agents given. Each noun is to be used only once.

transporter	generators	violators	treaters
maker	disposers	director	

1. Hercules sold its plant to another herbicide _____ .
2. Mr. Richard Hanneman, _____ of government affairs for the Solid Wastes Management Association, says the organization's membership is profiting from the RCRA.
3. EPA is trying to find _____ of the hazardous waste laws.

4. When a generator wants his waste removed, he gives it to a _____ for delivery to a disposer.
5. Because of the new laws, the companies that create wastes, the _____, are held liable for health and environmental risks.
6. The _____ of wastes are going to have difficulty finding sites for waste disposal in the future.
7. The General Accounting Office says that in the future, _____ of waste may be able to detoxify chemicals or change them into benign materials.

2. Structural Review

Causing someone to act

The three most common American verbs for expressing the idea of causing someone to act or something to happen are *make*, *have*, and *get*. *Make* and *have* follow the same sentence pattern and can be found in any tense:

		SUBJECT	VERB	NOUN/ PRONOUN	INFINITIVE (without *to*)
Example 1:	*make*	The EPA	made	Hercules	share the clean-up costs.
Example 2:	*have*	The generator	had	his lawyer	consider an EPA storage permit.

The verb *make* in Example 1 has the sense of *force* or *compel*. The meaning is strong, and you should use it only when it is a question of using force or strong pressure on someone to do something.

The verb *have* (*had* in Example 2) has the meaning of an order or requirement, especially of requiring something of someone who is being paid to do it or whose normal duty it is: "I'll *have* the transporter come take those cans away tomorrow."

The sentence pattern for *get* is a little different:

		SUBJECT	VERB	NOUN/ PRONOUN	INFINITIVE (with *to*)
Example 3:	*get*	Public opinion	got	Congress	to provide more protection.

The verb *get* (*got* in Example 3) means "persuade" or sometimes "influence," as one might influence or persuade a *partner* or *superior* to help. It is not usually a matter of force. Whereas you may *get* your boss to do something for you, it is unlikely that you will *make* him or *have* him do so, because this would mean that you have more control over him than is likely.

In summary, *make* is stronger than *have*, and *have* is stronger than *get*. Very often, however, *make* and *have* can be substituted for one another, as *have* and *get* can, since the meanings are rather similar.

In the following sentences, fill in the blanks with a correct form of *make*, *have*, or *get*. Write *to* in the parentheses before the infinitive only if it is necessary. Because the verbs are similar in meaning, there will often be more than one correct answer, but answer only once. Then discuss with the rest of the class or in small groups which of the three verbs make good answers and why.

1. In the '70s the EPA _____ Booz, Allen & Hamilton (   ) do a study of waste management industry revenues.
2. Recently, environmental groups _____ Mason Chemical (   ) declare its waste hazardous, even though the company was not obliged to do so.
3. Some say that Reagan's people would like to _____ the states (   ) enforce federal guidelines.
4. And Reagan may _____ Congress (   ) turn over the enforcement of waste handling regulation to the states.
5. But the National Solid Wastes Management Association hopes to _____ the Reagan administration (   ) keep the RCRA program much as it has been.
6. Many disposers fear that they cannot _____ communities (   ) permit hazardous dumps located nearby.
7. Some local environmental groups are trying to _____ their state governments (   ) bar interstate shipments.
8. In Colorado they are trying to _____ the legislature (   ) let each county decide for itself.
9. By means of a tremendous sales campaign, the industry is hoping to _____ the public (   ) understand that properly managed facilities offer no health risks.
10. Negative public opinion has _____ some facilities (   ) close their doors.
11. Small waste handlers have _____ their personnel (   ) study what can be done to stop larger companies from gobbling them up.

3. Business Communications

Note taking

Due to the nature of their work, people in business frequently attend meetings, carry on telephone conversations, or read lengthy reports. In each of these situations, the business person may want to take notes as a way of remembering the most important information. This chapter and Chapters Four and Five will introduce methods of note taking.

Read the example selection below. Then try to answer the questions by remembering the information you have just read. If you cannot remember the answers, look again at the selection. When you are finished, look over what you have done. Your answers are *notes on the most important information*. Notice that the notes are much shorter than the selection. When taking notes, you need not write complete sentences or worry about punctuation.

Example: In 1961, Hercules Inc. bought a onetime pesticide plant
in Arkansas and began manufacturing herbicides
including the infamous Agent Orange. Hercules tried to
dispose of wastes that were already on the plant site and
its own wastes. In 1971 Hercules leased and then sold the
site to another herbicide maker called Vertac Chemical
Corp. and has had nothing to do with the place since that
time.

Guiding Questions:
a. In 1961, who bought what?
b. What did Hercules do with wastes?
c. What did Hercules finally do with the plant and when?
d. What did Hercules do with the plant site after selling
it?

Answers (notes):
a. Hercules bought pesticide plant
b. disposed of wastes
c. sold plant in 1971
d. nothing to do with plant since 1971

Now read the selections below and take notes by answering the questions.

1. Hercules sold its herbicide plant in 1971 to Vertac. In 1980 laws were passed
that held waste generators liable for health and environmental risks and that
required wastes to be cleaned up. Also in 1980, Hercules had to pay part of the
expenses of cleaning up the wastes, even though the laws did not exist when
Hercules sold the plant in 1971.
   a. What two important events occurred in 1980?

2. In 1976 the Resource Conservation and Recovery Act (RCRA) was passed.
This is a law that regulates the disposal of hazardous wastes. The RCRA has
created a large amount of business for the waste-disposal industry, one which is
already growing rapidly. This industry takes upon itself the responsibility for
transporting, treating, and disposing of hazardous wastes. The disposal of wastes
is accomplished in cooperation with the EPA and similar state agencies. As the
laws for disposing of wastes get tougher, the waste-disposal industry will benefit.
   a. What important law is mentioned here and what kind of law is it?
   b. Who is helped by the law and what is their business?
   c. Who will be helped by even tougher laws?

3. Before the 1960s, the waste industry was only an "ordinary trash business."
Since the 1960s, the trash business has become a modern industry. The business
was transformed because of growing public opinion which demanded more protection for public health and the environment. Congress responded to public
opinion by passing environmental laws such as the Solid Waste Act of 1965 and
the Resource Conservation and Recovery Act of 1976, the latter requiring control of unusual and hazardous wastes.
   a. What kind of change took place in the trash business and when?
   b. Why did Congress create new laws?

4. The RCRA has established a set of regulations for the disposal of hazardous wastes. As a part of these, the EPA has classified about 200 substances as hazardous, and waste generators can consult this list to determine if they are liable for creating hazardous waste, or they can declare their wastes on their own if they believe them to be so. Every generator, transporter, treater, storer, or disposer of these wastes must notify EPA of that fact and get an EPA identification number, which must be used in any hazardous waste transaction. All of them must report to EPA annually on how much waste they handled and how they handled it.
   a. Who or what created the regulations?
   b. How do generators know if they may be liable for a waste?
   c. What is reported to the EPA and how often?

4. Action

Panel discussion

A panel is a group of people, each representing a different interest or opinion, who meet together publicly to discuss one topic or issue of interest to the audience. Panels are frequently seen on TV news programs. Usually a journalist leads the discussion by directing questions to the various members of the panel and by encouraging different members to reply to the answers given by the others.

Divide the class into small groups to discuss the disposal of hazardous waste. Each student should take the role of one of these panel members:

1. A *legislator* who is worried about public opinion of health and environmental risks and the dangers of dump sites.
2. Another *legislator* who supports business interests and who is troubled by governmental regulations and RCRA. He feels that the laws make it more difficult for business to serve the public, since more regulation means higher prices to the consumer.
3. An *executive* from Hercules who believes that his company's experience in 1980 was very unfair.
4. An *administrator* from the Solid Wastes Management Association who supports RCRA and enforcement of the law. He knows that tougher laws mean more business for members of his association.
5. A *journalist* who takes no sides on the issue and who asks questions to all panel members. He wants to discover facts that will interest his readers.

Each panel member should spend about five minutes preparing what he or she wants to communicate to the public before the discussion begins.

5. Reaction

Questions for discussion

1. Cases like that of Hercules Inc. are representative of a trend. Hercules sold its plant in 1971, yet in 1980, when new laws were passed, Hercules had to pay for the clean-up of the plant site. Do you think this is proper? Should Hercules be liable for actions which were still legal in 1971? What does this indicate about the relationship between government and business in the United States?

2. The Superfund is made up of money from both taxes and the chemical industry. Since this fund is used to clean up wastes created by chemical or chemical-related businesses, should tax money be used? Shouldn't all of the money be provided by the chemical industry, since some experts claim that the best way to encourage businesses to stop hazardous wastes is to make them pay for their own clean-up?

3. Because of numerous laws, the disposal of wastes is becoming very expensive. Are there too many regulations being placed upon businesses? Shouldn't the government only make suggestions about the disposal of wastes and offer to help businesses (rather than take them to court) in disposing of wastes? Remember, all expenses are eventually paid by the consumer, whether through taxes or higher prices.

SOCIAL ISSUES

CHAPTER THREE: Wounded Executives Fight Back on Age Bias

Business Week

Bias: prejudice, unfair and negative opinion of something.

Discrimination: unfair treatment (the result of bias).
Dynamic: active, energetic.
Actuarial: statistical, pertaining to the study of rates of occurrence of events.
Retirement: permanent ending of employment (usually because of age).
Perceived: sensed, having gained an awareness of.
Pension: regular payment made to someone old, disabled, widowed, or to an employee after long service.
Liabilities: debts, financial responsibilities.
Achievers: persons who accomplish something, especially something difficult.
Tempting: creating a desire.
Option: choice, alternative.
Recessionary: pertaining to a general economic slowdown.
To trim: to cut off a little bit of.
Invoking: calling on for help.
Act: group of related laws passed at the same time.
Suits: court actions, court cases.
Subsidiary: a company with more than 50% of the stock owned by another company.
Settled: reached an agreement, finished deciding.
Demoted: reduced in rank or to a lower position and pay.
Promotions: increases in rank or to higher positions and pay.
Pending: not yet settled or decided. In a court of law, a case which is "pending" is one which has been heard by the judge, but about which a decision has not yet been announced.

Age **discrimination** has long been a fact of corporate life in the U.S. Wall Street's emphasis on "youthful, **dynamic** management" and the **actuarial*** costs of an older staff have shortened many an executive's career. For some companies, firing or forcing early **retirement** on highly paid older executives has two **perceived*** advantages: It cuts salary costs and **pension liabilities*** and, at the same time, makes room at the top for young **achievers**. It is a particularly **tempting* option** in a **recessionary*** period like the present, when corporations seek to **trim** expenses.

But these days it is also a potentially costly option. Executives have begun to fight back by **invoking** the protections* of the 1967 Age Discrimination in Employment **Act** (ADEA). Among the companies that have recently lost **suits** under that act are Sandia Laboratories (a **subsidiary*** of Western Electric), in Albuquerque; Eastern Air Lines, in Miami; Chemetron, in Chicago; Atlantic Container Lines, in New York City; and Textron, in Providence.

Other companies have **settled** out of court. Standard Oil Co. of California paid $2 million to 264 employees in a 1974 age bias case. Pan American World Airways Inc. settled $900,000 on some 600 older management employees in 1978. Hartford Fire Insurance Co. (now Hartford Insurance Company), a subsidiary of International Telephone & Telegraph Corp., paid $240,000 last year to 72 current or former employees allegedly fired, **demoted**, or denied **promotions*** in violation* of the ADEA. And Connecticut General Insurance Corp. of Bloomfield, Conn., has quietly settled a number of individual age bias claims, with others **pending**.

No *fanfare*

Age bias has become a major corporate **issue** without the fanfare of earlier race and sex discrimination cases. However, few executives outside the companies involved know that age bias cases are pending against Consolidated Edison (in a suit that involves more than 150 managerial employees), National Broadcasting, Trans World, Japan Air Lines, Home Insurance, and Equitable Life Assurance.

In all such cases, say lawyers and management **consultants***, the **odds** are heavily in favor of the employee, particularly since **amendments** to the ADEA in 1978 assured the availability of jury trials. "When you put a large corporation against an employee in front of a **jury** on an issue like this, there is rarely any question as to the outcome," says George P. Sape, vice-president of Organization Resource Counselors Inc., a New York–based **employee relations*** consultant.

In Connecticut, two former **officers*** of Bloomfield-based Kaman Corp. have **sued** to recover income and benefits lost when they were fired in 1978. The men—a $90,000-a-year president of a subsidiary and a $50,000-a-year director of corporate affairs—were both nearing age 60. They claim that there is a decade-long pattern of discrimination at Kaman that has ended the careers of more than two dozen executives in their 50s and has prevented any corporate officer from reaching what was formerly the normal retirement age of 65. The company **denies** all charges but **declines** further comment.

Clearly, there is a national trend. V. Paul Donnelly, a Detroit **attorney***, claims to have age discrimination cases pending or in court against at least 150 major corporations. He says: "I'm finding guys coming in now from all over, in the $60,000-and-up range, presidents and high vice-presidents. If people at those levels start talking, they can cause big problems for corporations."

"In the next decade," says Leonard S. Janofsky, president of the American Bar Assn., "the age act (ADEA) will be the source of a great percentage of employment discrimination **litigation**, perhaps even eclipsing Title VII (which covers race and sex)." Since July [1979], the **EEOC** has recorded 8,000 complaints, nearly double the number of the previous year.

The number of age bias suits filed by individuals is believed to be up, although the 1979 figure is unavailable because the EEOC does not record private suits. In 1978, when the Labor Dept. kept track, more than 400 private suits were filed, many of them by executives with enough savings to wait out such litigation.

Special obligation

"Age discrimination is not only widespread but it is widely accepted by many Americans who have rejected discrimination based on race and sex," EEOC Chair Eleanor Holmes Norton told the House Select Committee on Aging last month. Because of this at-

Fanfare: exaggerated publicity.

Issue: question for discussion.

Consultants: experts who are hired for a short time to provide knowledge or advice.
Odds: probability.
Amendments: formal changes.
Jury: group of citizens who decide guilt or innocence during a trial.
Employee relations: dealings between management and employees.

Officers: persons with a position of authority.
Sued: brought suit.
Denies: says (something) is not true.
Declines: refuses (politely).

Attorney: lawyer.

Litigation: court action, legal activity.
EEOC: Equal Employment Opportunity Commission.

David G. Klein

Courts are ruling against employers in age bias cases.

Intention: aim, purpose.

Demographics: statistics based on large populations, or characteristics of large groups.
Labor force: the working population of a country or region.
Post-: after (added at the beginning of a word).
Postwar: after the war.
Middle-management: pertaining to management positions which are neither the highest ones nor the lowest ones.
Upward mobility: capability of movement to a higher position.

titude, the EEOC feels a special obligation to move aggressively on these cases, Norton said. She explained that the agency aims to demonstrate to employers their **intention*** to actively enforce the law.

U.S. **demographics** suggest that the agency's attorneys will have plenty to do. By 1985, 36% of the **labor force*** will be more than 40 years of age. Meanwhile, members of the **postwar** baby boom—many of them now adults in **middle-management*** ranks—will be pushing for the higher-level jobs held by executives in their late 40s and 50s. "As talent becomes more plentiful and there's a real need for **upward mobility***, companies will say that the easiest way to accomplish it will be to retire older managers," says Dilworth F. Brown, senior vice-president of Meidinger Inc., a consulting firm based in Louisville.

"We're suggesting to corporations that they must use a **due-process***" approach," says H. Reeve Darling, president of Los Angeles Consulting Group. "They've got to be able to demonstrate measurable differences in **performance**, and employees must be reviewed at several levels." Darling adds that "right now, there is probably not a company in this country that has an adequate and effective **appraisal** program **in place**."

Due-process: pertaining to fair, timely, and legal action.
Performance: quality of work.
Appraisal: evaluation, judging.
In place: functioning, in operation.

Self-protection

Likewise, the former employees' attorneys are also providing advice for endangered executives. "They should be aware of the law and the signs," says one. "A sophisticated employer who wants to get rid of an older, too-highly paid executive nowadays is going to do it in a subtle way over a period of time by building up a **dossier** on little ways he **screwed up**. If the executive senses he is getting out of favor, he should start building his own dossier, keep notes and copies of **commendations***, and, most of all, do a good job."

Dossier: collection of various papers for a specific purpose, especially for showing and describing the qualifications of a candidate for a job.
Screwed up: made a mistake (sometimes considered very impolite).
Commendations: compliments, praise.

Because the ADEA has a six-month **deadline*** for filing a claim of age discrimination—although in states with their own age bias agencies, the deadline is extended to 300 days—employees who feel that age was the sole reason for their **discharge** should move fast, advises Donnelly.

Deadline: last acceptable time that something must be done.
Discharge: being fired, dismissal (of an employee).

Some companies give a discharged older employee six months' pay "so that the man will forget about filing an age discrimination claim until after the 180 days are up," Donnelly says. Similarly, he cautions, the hiring of counselors to help discharged **white-collar*** workers find new employment may be designed mainly to use up the six-month filing period.

White-collar: pertaining to those who do not work with their hands (from the fact that office workers traditionally wore white shirts).

In addition to federal suits, state courts have helped the older employee who feels that his dismissal is because of his age. In Michigan, the state Supreme Court ruled that both Masco Corp. and Blue Cross & Blue Shield of Michigan had entered into an implied agreement with their employees by emphasizing pension plans and job security in their recruiting material; therefore, the court said, the organizations must show "**just cause***" before **depriving*** an employee of those benefits. This marks a change in the traditional doctrine that nonunion white-collar workers can be fired **at will***. "The company is selling itself, too, when it hires people," Donnelly says. "What those rulings say is that a company must be **bound** by the promises it makes."

Just cause: legal and fair reason.
Depriving: taking away from.
At will: arbitrarily, at any time, whenever one likes.
Bound: put under legal obligation, made liable.

1. Business Vocabulary

A. In English, nouns and verbs frequently share the same base (root). Many verbs may add the ending *-ion* (or often *-tion*, or *-ation*) to form a noun:

create   creation

Notice that the final *-e* of the verb disappears in the noun form. In every case, the ending *-ion* means "process," "act," or "state of being." *Creation* is the act of creating, or it is what has been created.

Look at the following examples from the article of verbs which can be made into nouns by adding some form of *-ion*.

VERB	NOUN
protect (from)	protection (from)
intend	intention
promote	promotion
violate	violation
deprive (of)	deprivation (of)
commend	commendation
tempt	temptation
perceive	perception

To familiarize yourself with both verbs and nouns and their meanings, write the verb form of the word beside its meaning in the list below.

1. _____ to gain understanding, to realize
2. _____ to keep something from someone
3. _____ to guard, to keep from danger
4. _____ to raise to a more important job or rank
5. _____ to have a purpose in mind
6. _____ to praise, to approve of
7. _____ to break a rule or law
8. _____ to create a desire (often a desire for something bad)

Now write the noun form next to its meaning:

9. _____ the act of approving, praising
10. _____ the act of breaking a law or rule
11. _____ the result or process of gaining understanding
12. _____ the fact of having a purpose in mind
13. _____ the act of keeping something from someone
14. _____ an advancement in job or rank
15. _____ the act of keeping from danger
16. _____ the creation of a desire

From among the sixteen forms you have written, choose the one which is appropriate for each blank in the following memo.

MEMORANDUM

Date: November 23, 19—
To: Robert Ellison
From: Deborah Weaver
Subject: Age Bias

I have just read a recent magazine article in *Business Week* which discusses age bias in business. The article comments on the fact that many businesses _____ the rights of many older managers in business by not giving them a _____ as they approach sixty-five years of age and by cutting their pensions. Companies are frequently _____ to fire older executives or to force them to retire early.

However, many of the affected businessmen are seeking the _____ of the 1967 Age Discrimination in Employment Act (ADEA). Under this law, any business which has _____ a person of his/her job and pension benefits may be in _____ of the law and can be sued by the person affected. The Equal Employment Opportunity Commission _____ to enforce the law whenever possible.

Robert, please check the personnel files on all our departments' older employees. Find out if any have been given a written _____ for good work within the last three years or if any have been _____ to a higher position within the last two years. It is not the _____ of this department to _____ older managers of any legal rights.

Please report your findings within the week. Thanks.

B. Choose the most appropriate word from the following list to complete the sentences.

white collar	subsidiary
officers	liabilities
recession	actuarial
labor force	attorney
deadline	consultants

1. _____ costs of an older staff have helped to shorten many an executive's career.
2. Early retirement helps the company by cutting salary costs and other _____.
3. During a period of _____, early retirement of older executives is especially appealing to corporations.
4. Sandia Laboratories is a _____ of Western Electric.
5. Management _____ say employees who have been discriminated against have a good chance of winning in court because the trials are jury trials.
6. Executives are frequently called _____.
7. A lawyer may also be referred to as an _____.
8. By 1985, 36% of the _____ will be more than 40 years of age.
9. Some state agencies are extending the _____ for filing a claim of age discrimination.
10. Sometimes, corporations hire counselors to help discharged _____ workers.

C.   The meanings of many two-word phrases may seem obvious, because each word in the phrase is a familiar one. But, together, the words may have a special meaning. This chapter includes several two-word phrases which are frequently used in business.

From the list below, fill in each blank with the most appropriate two-word phrase.

employee relations	middle management
due process	upward mobility
labor force	just cause
at will	

Many companies fire or force early retirement on highly paid older executives. Employees are fighting back, saying that nonunion white-collar workers cannot be fired _____ and that any company which wants to fire an employee must first show _____ .

Age bias is partly a result of the large number of younger executives. As the number of younger, _____ level executives increases, the need for _____ increases. This may become a greater problem as more of the _____ grows older.

This problem of age bias has created business for specialists in _____ . These people consult with both businesses and employees. Presently, they are advising businesses to observe _____ of law when preparing to fire someone.

2. Structural Review

Expressing custom or repeated action in the past: *used to*

Used to + INFINITIVE expresses custom and habit, repeated action, or permanent state in the past. There is nothing like it in the present.

Examples:	Custom and habit:	Companies *used to* look for employees with lots of experience.
	Repeated action:	One corporation *used to* fire one older executive after another.
	Permanent state:	Before 1967 and the ADEA, many older management employees *used to* see little hope of fighting back.

Often, *used to* is employed to contrast something in the past with a new condition in the present.

Negative. In American English the negative is *didn't use to* (or *did not use to* in formal language).

Questions. In American English, *used to* is treated like a normal "do" verb:

Did you used to worry about being fired?
You used to come in early, *didn't* you?

Pronunciation. The "s" in *used to* is pronounced /s/, not /z/.

Notice that *to be used to*, meaning *to be accustomed to*, has nothing to do with *used to* + INFINITIVE discussed above.

The following phrases can be combined into sentences if you add *used to*. Add only *used to*. No other words are necessary for the formation of a good sentence. This exercise is easy if you read all the parts and then look for the subject of the sentence.

1. age discrimination cases / very few / be taken to court
2. before ADEA / be helpless / older management employees
3. white collar workers / their own companies / sue / never
4. be low / brought by individuals / age bias suits / the number of
5. older white-collar workers / have more faith in / their own companies / in
6. to move older executives out / be less pressure / there
7. in firing older executives / there was no danger / to feel that / corporations

3. Business Communications

Note taking and summarization

Chapter One has introduced the idea that a summary is a short, orderly collection of the most important information in an article. It is different from notes, since it is written in sentence form. The ability to summarize is very useful to busy people. To do it well, you must understand the information and decide what is most important.

Look back at note taking in Chapter Two. There you took notes on short selections by writing answers to the questions in only a few words. For each selection, if you combine the notes and put them into sentence form, you will have a summary. Using the example in Chapter Two, p. 21, and expanding the notes, we have a summary sentence:

> Hercules bought a pesticide plant and disposed of its wastes. Hercules sold the plant in 1971 and has had no involvement in the plant since that time.

You can take notes on and write a summary of an entire article simply by asking yourself questions like those in Chapter Two.

Now, read the selections given below, decide what questions need to be asked, and write the answers in note form. When you finish making notes on all the selections, put all the notes together in sentence form in one paragraph. Now you will have completed a summary of the selections.

1. Age discrimination has long been a fact of corporate life in the U.S. The business community has emphasized youthful, dynamic management. For many companies, firing or forcing early retirement on highly paid older executives has two perceived advantages: it cuts salary costs and pension liabilities, and it makes room at the top for young achievers.
2. These days it is a potentially costly option. Executives have begun to fight back by invoking the protections of the 1967 Age Discrimination in Employment Act. Many companies have gone to court and have lost suits. Other companies have paid large amounts of money to settle out of court.

3. Age bias has become a major corporate issue because many companies have lawsuits filed against them, and the odds are in favor of the employee. The lawsuits are decided by jury trials, and this is what gives the employee an advantage. Examples of this are Standard Oil Co. of California which paid $2 million to 264 employees in a 1974 age bias case, Pan American World Airways, Inc., which paid $900,000 to 600 older management employees; and the Hartford Fire Insurance Co. which paid $240,000 to seventy-two employees.

4. The Equal Employment Opportunity Commission (EEOC) is very concerned about age discrimination because many Americans accept this sort of discrimination, even though they do not accept sexual or racial discrimination. The EEOC plans to demonstrate to employers their intention actively to enforce the law.

5. The EEOC will probably have plenty to do because by 1985, 36% of the labor force will be over 40 years of age. Also, members of the postwar baby boom will be moving into middle-management positions and will be pushing for the higher-level jobs held by executives in their late 40s and 50s. Companies will be wanting to retire older managers so the young can move up.

4. Action

An exit interview

Interviewing is an extremely useful method for communicating in business. Interviews are not only used by personnel departments in deciding which applicant to hire, but also used by managers in evaluating worker performance and job satisfaction. An interview may also be conducted with workers who are involved in disciplinary problems. Managers use exit interviews to understand why workers leave the company. A large amount of information may be exchanged in an interview; therefore, business people must be familiar with the types of questions regularly used in interviews.

Questions, of course, are the essence of interviews. Questions and their answers keep the interview moving. The person conducting the interview (the interviewer) controls the interview by skillfully using various types of questions. Some questions are open and others are closed, some are neutral while others direct the interviewee's response in a specific direction. Two other question types are based on what the interviewee says: mirror questions and searching questions. Both of these questions ask the interviewee to elaborate on the previous response given by the interviewee. These are explained below.

Open and closed questions

Open questions. These questions allow the interviewee the greatest amount of freedom when answering. They are usually broad or general questions which only specify the topic the interviewee is to discuss. Examples of these questions are:

How would you describe yourself?
What do you consider to be your greatest strengths
    and weaknesses?
How do you determine or evaluate success?

This type of questioning has the advantage of providing the interviewer the opportunity of observing the interviewee in a situation that does not threaten the interviewee. However, the answer to the question can become lengthy and time-consuming, and the interviewer loses some control over the interview situation.

Closed questions. These questions are more limited and, therefore, the response is usually briefer than with open questions. These questions limit the interviewee's possible range of answers. Examples of closed questions are:

> Which is more important to you, the money or the type of job?
> Will you relocate? Does relocation bother you?
> How do you work under pressure?

With these questions, anyone can conduct the interview; a trained interviewer is not needed. Also, the interview can be conducted in less time with these questions, and the interviewer has more control over the interview.

Usually, a combination of open and closed questions is needed to obtain the maximum amount of information and to allow for uninhibited communication while minimizing the time required for conducting the interview.

Non-neutral and neutral questions

Non-neutral questions. Questions may also put pressure on the interviewee to answer in a certain direction. These are useful when trying to verify factual information. Some questions put less pressure on the interviewee than do others as the following examples show:

> You do type, don't you?
> What do you think of big government's needless waste of money?
> How do you feel about this company's foolish sick leave policy?

All three of these questions can trap the interviewee into answering in a certain direction. The last two are more forceful than the first. These should be used only by a skillful interviewer.

Neutral questions. Neutral questions do not put pressure on the interviewee. These are the most commonly used questions. Responses to these questions are usually more accurate than are responses to questions which put pressure on the interviewee. Examples of neutral questions are:

> In what ways do you think you can contribute to this company?
> In what kind of work environment are you most comfortable?

Neutral questions are usually used because they require an accurate, nonpressured response.

Mirror questions and searching questions

Mirror questions. These questions use the exact words an interviewee used in responding to a question. Mirror questions try to get extra information about the previous responses to a question. Examples of the mirror question are:

> Interviewee: I like my present job, but I don't get along with my
>   boss.
>
> Interviewer: You don't get along with your boss?

Interviewee: I liked the work, but it took too many hours.

Interviewer: It took too many hours?

These questions reflect the wording used by the interviewee for the purpose of getting a more complete answer.

Searching questions. Like the mirror question, the searching question seeks more information about the interviewee's previous response. The difference is that the question does not use the same wording. Examples of this type of question are:

Interviewee: In my last job, I learned how to supervise the work of others.

Interviewer: How many people did you supervise?
What was your role as supervisor?
How long did you supervise this work?

In both the searching question and the mirror question, the questions are not planned before the interview. These are questions which the interviewer thinks of while conducting the interview.

The six question types discussed above make up the basic question types used in any type of interview. By planning the interview ahead of time and getting a plan for the sort of questions you want to ask, you should be able to get the maximum amount of information from any interview you conduct.

Break the class into groups of three. Suppose that one member of the group is being fired from his or her job and that the other members of the group are representatives of their companies. The employee is being fired primarily because of his or her age, but the company does not want to admit that this is the primary reason.

The representatives of the company should explain all of the reasons that the person is being fired, including mistakes made on the job. The employee should inquire if the real reason is because of his or her age and should argue that the mistakes mentioned by the company are not enough reason to be fired.

The employee and company representative may want to consider the following:

a. The company might give the employee extra pay when he leaves the company. The amount can be discussed.
b. The employee has been paying for insurance while working for the company for many years. Perhaps he can continue his insurance even after he leaves the company.
c. The company can help him find another job. What sort of job would he find, and would the pay be as good as his present pay?
d. The employee can threaten to sue under the ADEA and take the company to court. This could cost the company a great deal of money.
e. The employee can threaten to sue, and the company can agree to settle out of court. The representative and the employee can discuss the settlement.

Each member of the group should make a list of the questions to be asked. Then each group should conduct the interview before the class. The members of the class should observe the interviews and note the types of questions being used and how successful the group is in getting the information they wanted. After each interview, discuss the questions used and why they were used. Discuss whether or not other types of questions would have been better.

5. Reaction

Questions for discussion

1. Which is more important, the energy of a youthful employee or the wisdom and experience of an older one? Which is more expensive?
2. What chance does an older executive have if his company decides he should be discharged? What can he do to prepare for such an event? What kind of compromise can be reached between the older executive and his company?
3. What is the attitude of people in your country toward older members of society, both in general and in business? Do businesses consider them a liability or an asset, and why?
4. What are the solutions that are applied in other countries to this problem? Is it necessary for older executives frequently to have to sue their own companies? Who will benefit from this constant litigation? Who benefits most when the older executive leaves?

CHAPTER FOUR: **Earning an Undergraduate Degree At the Plant**

Business Week

Associate's degree: a degree received after two years of college work after high school graduation.
Cornerstone: basic building block in the foundation of a building; basis.
Premises: land and the buildings on it.

To pick up: begin again.
Left off: stopped (doing something), ceased.

To proliferate: to grow, to reproduce.
In-house: within the plant or company.

Peter E. Weissgarber, 38, a general foreman at the Electric Boat Div. of General Dynamics Corp. in Groton, Conn., is the first of five sons in his family to earn a college degree. On July 11, [1980,] Weissgarber was among 44 Electric Boat employees to receive an **associate's degree** in business administration from the University of New Haven's "**Cornerstone**" program, in which undergraduate degrees may be earned entirely on the employer's **premises**.

A similar program conducted by High Point College at the offices of R.J. Reynolds Industries Inc. in Winston-Salem, N.C., is enabling JoAnn Sprink, 43, an export coordinator for cigarettes, to **pick up** where she **left off** 20 years ago. Then, she had quit college to get married and raise a family. Now, she is studying for a bachelor's degree in business administration and enjoys the convenience of going to classes where she works.

Such undergraduate degree programs have begun to **proliferate*** at large companies across the U.S. Graduate degree programs in management, finance, engineering and other specialties have long been offered **in-house*** by a small group of companies, including TRW, Fluor, Monsanto, Digital Equipment, Bechtel, some divisions of General Motors, and Ford Motor, but most of the undergraduate degree programs are new.

Probably fewer than 5% of companies with 500 or more employees offer them today, says Washington's National Institute for Work & Learning (NIWL, formerly the National Manpower Institute), but the number is increasing fast. The trend serves the mutual interests of colleges faced with declining campus enrollments through the 1980s, companies seeking to broaden the education of their workers, and employees who lack either money or time to pursue higher education on their own.

"This is the trend of the future," says Donald W. Fletcher, associate dean for **extended*** education at California State University & Colleges (CSUC). "It makes sense to offer courses where students are, especially because of the energy crisis." CSUC is currently **negotiating*** with Rockwell International Corp. to offer courses at its Los Angeles **facility***.

Says John W. Jordan, dean of Northeastern University's college for part-time students in Boston: "Industry has the needs, and universities have the expertise. We might as well put them together."

Although **future-oriented***, some of the on-site programs grew out of a very old kind of education: **apprenticeship** training. At United Technologies' Pratt & Whitney Aircraft Group in East Hartford, the five-year-old associate's degree program **stemmed from** a three-year, 30-**credit** apprenticeship program conducted at the plant by Manchester Community College.

Expanding

Employees who had gone through the program and **sought** to complete work toward a degree on the outside found that colleges required a **frustrating*** amount of **duplication***. So the company contracted with Manchester to provide 30 additional **liberal arts** credits on-site. Now it is expanding the program to three other Connecticut plants through community colleges in those areas and has concentrated with Eastern Connecticut State College in Willimantic to offer a bachelor of science degree in business administration.

One of the largest in-house degree programs is the eight-year-old one available to employees of Digital Equipment Corp., the rapidly growing, $2.3 billion minicomputer manufacturer in Maynard, Mass. Teachers from three area universities—Boston University, Worcester Polytechnic Institute, and Clark University—travel to Maynard, where employees may earn degrees ranging from a B.S. in business administration to an M.B.A. or a master's degree in electrical engineering. Teachers from the University of New Hampshire teach undergraduate degree courses at DEC's facilities in Merrimack, N.H. In all, some 2,000 of the 7,000 employees participating in DEC's **tuition reimbursement*** program are taking courses on-site.

In-house hiring

Such courses play a particularly **vital*** role at high-technology companies such as DEC, says Robert R. Clark, manager of corporate management and **employee development** for the company. "With our hiring **demands**, the more people we develop in-house, the better," he says.

At Electric Boat, too, the program fills specific needs because the University of New Haven has **tailored** it to a shipbuilding environment. The required science courses, for example, include one in radiation safety—**eminently** practical in a shipyard where nuclear submarines are built. Cornerstone's management and market-

Extended: here, not on the college campus, off-campus.
Negotiating: trying to reach an agreement on price and terms.
Facility: installation, plant.

Oriented: with an attitude toward; conscious, aware.
Future-oriented: conscious of and prepared for the future.
Apprenticeship: the practice of working with another person for a number of years in order to learn a trade.
Stemmed from: grew out of, came from.
Credit: unit which can be counted toward a college degree.

Sought (past tense of seek): tried to.
Frustrating: irritating, disappointing because of the prevention of fulfillment of one's plans.
Duplication: copying, doing the same thing more than once.
Liberal arts: area of college or university study which is of a general nature, covering preliminary study in a broad range of fields.

Tuition: entry fee for colleges or universities.
Reimbursement: paying back (money).

Vital: crucial, absolutely necessary.
Employee development: a systematic effort to improve the qualifications or abilities of the employees.
Demands: needs.

Tailored: made (for) specially.
Eminently: outstandingly, extremely.

Recent graduates beam while receiving University of New Haven undergraduate degrees.

Entrepreneurial: having to do with the individual who goes out on his own to start or run a business.

OSHA: Occupational Safety and Health Administration.

Mounted: usually, went up; here, set up, initiated, began.

Accommodated: served, provided for, welcomed.

ing courses deal with large corporate scenarios rather than the **entrepreneurial** approach. The business law course puts strong emphasis on contracts, labor law, and **OSHA** and EEOC requirements.

Both DEC and Electric Boat **mounted** vigorous selling campaigns to persuade colleges to export professors and support personnel to job sites. But many other in-house programs are the result of aggressive marketing by colleges.

"It was a bit of a selling job," says High Point Dean M. Murphy Osborne. Reynolds officials liked the idea, but were skeptical that enough would want on-site education to make it worthwhile. To their surprise, more than 900 employees responded positively to a survey. When five undergraduate programs were offered last September, 300 employees—more than twice the number that could be **accommodated**—signed up for the courses.

Few support services

Not all colleges approve of job-site degree programs. Robert F. Bahnsen, assistant to the president of the Hartford Graduate Center of Rensselaer Polytechnic Institute, thinks that such programs may have "too few **support functions**, such as libraries and laboratories, on the premises." Ronald R. Gist, acting dean at the University of Denver's College of Business Administration, fears that off-campus programs might endanger the university's educational **accreditation** because "we would be placing the matter of **admission** in the hands of the company, not the school."

Universities that do cooperate in on-site programs deny that any such **abdication** takes place. "Complete academic control remains with the individual academic departments on campus," says Richard C. Morrison, dean of the School of Professional Studies & Continuing Education at the University of New Haven. Morrison and other educators insist that students must **meet** university requirements. In fact, many of the 1,200 employees at GMC Truck & Coach Div. who were interested in its on-site undergraduate program failed to meet the University of Detroit's admissions standards.

Convenience **draws*** many employees to on-site college programs, but **compatibility** with their fellow students also **attracts*** them, say participants. As John E. Cunningham, education and training coordinator for First Pennsylvania Bank, explains it, "These courses are aimed mainly at people who might have **anxiety over** college courses, people who don't know if they can handle college, or people over 35, who say, 'I don't want to go on a campus with those kids.'" Says Jean P. Leca, 39, supervisor in the operations department at Electric Boat: "I'm too old for that **rah-rah, pom-pom stuff**."

No more vouchers

Most companies require employees to pay for the on-site programs and then reimburse 75% to 100% of the tuitions upon successful completion of the courses. Until recently, Ford Motor Co. gave employees **vouchers** for courses, and CMU subsequently **billed*** the company. On July 1 this was **discontinued***. As a result, Ford **enrollment*** in the program dropped from 375 in February to 275 at latest count. In Electric Boat's program, however, the employee pays no money **up front**, and that is a strong **incentive** to enroll.

The companies, too, have an important **stake** in such programs, says P. Takis Veliotis, executive vice-president for **marine** affairs at General Dynamics and general manager of Electric Boat. At EB, he reports, the education program has increased employee loyalty, reduced **turnover***, improved **productivity*** and the quality of **supervision***, and **enhanced*** the company's **recruiting*** efforts.

Employees seem equally convinced of the program's benefits. EB's Weissgarber is sure that Cornerstone helped win his recent promotion from pipe-fitting supervisor to general foreman. "They selected me for two reasons," he says. "One, I was rated No. 1 in my department in performance as a supervisor. And two, I had the education."

Support functions: activities or programs that give help.
Accreditation: license, official approval, authorization.
Admission: the process of deciding who is allowed to enter the college.

Abdication: giving up of power or responsibility.
Meet (requirements, standards): here, satisfy.

Draws: here, attracts, pulls in.
Compatibility: ease in getting along with.
Attracts: pulls towards (by unseen force); gets the attention of; creates interest or pleasure in.
Anxiety over: worry about.
Rah-rah, pom-pom stuff: Imitative of young college students' football yells; characterized by excessive juvenile enthusiasm.

Vouchers: documents showing that payment has been made in advance.
Billed: sent a written statement of charges for goods or services.
Discontinued: ceased, put an end to.
Enrollment: number of people who have signed up (for a program).
Up front: at the beginning, initially.
Incentive: reward, motive, reason to do something.

Stake: share or interest, usually financial.
Marine: related to water, especially transportation on water.
Turnover: replacement of personnel.
Productivity: rate or speed at which goods are manufactured or processed.
Supervision: Overseeing, watching and directing (employees of an organization).
Enhanced: made better, improved.
Recruiting: getting or enlisting persons as employees.

1. Business Vocabulary

A. Chapter Three showed you that some nouns that express an act or state of being are made from verbs. This was done by adding some form of *-ion* to the end of the verb. Thousands of these exist and are found in Chapter Four as well. Study the lists below.

Following see a letter of inquiry (a letter which asks for information) which needs to be completed. Fill in the blanks with a correct form of the verb or noun from the list of words given.

VERBS	NOUNS
duplicate	duplication
attract	attraction
frustrate	frustration
negotiate	negotiation
extend	extension
discontinue	discontinuation
proliferate	proliferation
orient	orientation
supervise	supervision
produce	production

August 24, 19—

General Computers
4602 Gromberg Ln.
St. Louis, MO 32543

Freitan Industries
1241 Crescent St.
San Diego, CA 90032

Gentlemen:

I have been told that your company has a very successful in-house degree program for your employees. As this type of program seems to be _____ now, I would like to ask a few questions about yours.

First, I need to know how to deal with a school. My company wants to _____ many of our workers to the program, and we feel that successful _____ with the school will be important. Does such a program require a great deal of cooperation between the company and the school?

Also, I want to know about the workers themselves. I have read that in-house education makes better employees. Does your program in fact _____ better workers? Do they _____ their education, or do they continue their study at a college or university? I have also read that many students who try to continue their study at a college are often _____ by the amount of _____ in college courses of things they have learned on the job. I wonder if a brief _____ program at the beginning for all new students would help solve this problem?

Lastly, how does your company feel about these _____ courses? Do the courses raise the company's _____ or increase the quality of _____?

I realize that I have asked a number of questions. However, if you would help me with any information you may have, I would be very thankful.

Yours respectfully,

Charlene Gibbons
Employee Relations

B.   Circle the letter of the choice which best completes the sentence.
1. DEC, a high-technology company, has an *in-house* degree program. The program is located at
   a. the college campus.   b. its plant.   c. Chicago.
2. DEC *reimbursed* their employees for the money spent on tuition. The company
   a. gave money to the college.
   b. took the money out of the employees' pay.
   c. repaid the employees.
3. These courses play a *vital* role in high-technology companies. For these companies, educational programs are
   a. very important.   b. good publicity.   c. expensive.
4. Besides improving productivity and employee loyalty, these programs have reduced *turnover*. More employees are
   a. quitting.   b. studying.   c. staying with their jobs.
5. These companies advertise their educational programs when they are *recruiting*. The programs help the companies
   a. sell stock.   b. increase their capital.
   c. attract new employees.
6. Rockwell International Corp. might offer courses at its Los Angeles *facility*. If so, the course would be held at
   a. a school.   b. Rockwell's plant.   c. an office.
7. On-site college programs *draw* many employees. The programs
   a. educate employees.   b. discourage employees.
   c. attract employees.
8. Electric Boat's program requires no money up front, and that is a strong incentive to *enroll*. Programs like this make employees want to
   a. sign up.   b. quit.   c. work harder.
9. The Ford Motor Company had a degree program, and the college *billed* the company. Ford received a
   a. check.   b. letter.   c. request for payment.
10. Electric Boat found that its educational program *enhanced* the company's recruiting efforts. Recruitment was
   a. helped.   b. slowed.   c. made difficult.

2. Structural Review

**Expressing past events with a special connection to the present:
present perfect**

Look at the following sentence pattern:

SUBJECT + *have/has* + PAST PARTICIPLE + (VERB
                                                                        COMPLEMENT)

Example: A change   has   occurred   on the work-site.

The present perfect tense tells something about the past but is different from the simple past tense. A person using the simple past tense does not want to express anything about the connection with the present time. But when he uses the present perfect, he does intend to relate a past event to the present in one of two ways:

(1) Either the event in the past continues up to the present moment, or

(2) the event in the past has results that are important for the present moment.

In the example above, the work-site has changed in some way. It is still changed. The speaker wants to say that the change is *important for the present*. The result of the change exists in the present, and we must consider that fact.

Because the present perfect is the tense that allows a person to emphasize the *present* importance of a past event, specific indications of time are used only with the simple past tense, never with the present perfect. Some examples of specific indications of time are *last year*, *the other day*, *in 1981*, *yesterday*, and *on January 1*.

Example: *Last year* four employees received degrees.

Nevertheless, you should remember that if the time specified is not yet completed, the present perfect is the natural tense to use, because the event is continuous up to the moment of speaking.

Example: Three other employees have been in the program only
                    six months *so far*.

Other possibilities for time words with the present perfect tense are *this year*, *today*, *not yet*, *during the present century*, *for three months*, and *since Friday*.

In the following memo, decide which of the two tenses—present perfect or simple past—you would like to use to express the meaning implied in the passage. In only *two* of the blanks, *either* tense may be used; which do you think they are?

MEMO

Date: Feb. 12, 1981
To: Beverly Archibald
From: Tom Crowley
Subject: Background report for consideration
            of an on-site educational program
            here at Saftien Electronics

This memo is in response to your phone call of Feb. 2, requesting me to advise you on the current situation of on-site degree programs and to offer a recommendation as to how we might go about planning one for our high-tech facility.

As you (mention) _____ to me then, undergrad degree programs (begin) _____ to proliferate at large companies across the U.S. A small group of large companies (offer) _____ graduate specialties such as management, finance, and engineering since the 1960s, but about 1977, undergrad programs also (catch on) _____. During the last few years, the number (increase) _____ considerably, and both colleges and businesses (begin) _____ to see that benefits exist for everyone involved, and many now see in them "the trend of the future."

For example, five years ago, United Technologies (initiate) _____ an on-site program in East Hartford. Since then, the program (be) _____ a source of pride for the workers, who (gain) _____ a new sense of loyalty to their company as well.

However, most relevant to our own plans is Digital Equipment's program, which (start) _____ eight years ago and (grow) _____ considerably since that time.

Since for some time program administrators (see) _____ the necessity of relating the program to the needs of employees of a high-tech corporation like ours, I would recommend that we seriously consider investigating either program as a model for our own. They (gain) _____ a lot of excellent experience and (profit) _____ from it in both employee development and morale. They (have) _____ no greater resources then than we do now, so I can see no reason why we cannot do just as well.

I hope this is the kind of recommendation you (want) _____ when you (call) _____.

3. Business Communications

Note taking: The central idea

A good listener must try to organize information while listening. The listener should try to understand what information is the main idea and what information is of secondary importance.

Look at the example below, and choose the central idea from the three choices that are given.

> Example: Peter Weissgarber is the first of five sons in his family to earn a college degree. He received his degree in business administration and studied on the employer's premises. Such undergraduate degree programs are growing in number and are helping people like Peter get a college degree.
>
> a. Peter was the first son in his family to get a college degree.
> b. Such undergraduate degree programs are growing in number.
> c. Such undergraduate degree programs are helping people like Peter to get a college degree.

The answer is c.

Now look at the following selections and choose the central idea.

1. Although these programs are future oriented, some programs grew out of a very old kind of education: apprenticeship training. Many companies are just beginning to use the degree programs, but some companies such as the Pratt and Whitney Aircraft Group have a degree program because it first had an apprenticeship program.
   a. These degree programs are future oriented.
   b. Many companies are just now beginning to use these programs.
   c. Some programs have grown out of apprenticeship training.

2. Some people who studied on company premises had problems continuing their study outside the company at colleges. Many people found that colleges required a frustrating amount of duplication. Because of this problem, some schools are expanding the number of courses they offer on the job site.
   a. Some of the programs have actually been helped by the problems students found at colleges outside the company.
   b. Many students were frustrated by the amount of duplication required by colleges.
   c. The program is causing problems for some people.

3. Some companies, like DEC, feel that it is important to train people in-house. Both DEC and Electric Boat were so interested that they mounted sales campaigns to persuade colleges to export professors and support personnel to job sites. They like having courses tailored to the company's needs. These programs are particularly vital to these high-technology companies.
   a. DEC and Electric Boat had difficulty in getting degree programs to their companies.
   b. Some high-technology companies feel that these degree programs are vital to their companies.
   c. Courses are tailored to the companies' needs.

4. These degree programs lack many of the facilities of regular college study programs such as libraries and laboratories. Because of this, not all colleges approve of job-site programs. Also, some colleges worry that off-campus programs might endanger the university's educational accreditation because the

school can't control admissions. Other universities, however, say this is not true.

    a. Job-site programs do not have enough education facilities.

    b. Arguments against job-site degree programs are not always true.

    c. There are some problems with job-site degree programs.

Once you understand the central idea of a talk or of a written selection, you must discover the secondary ideas. Now go back to the four selections you have just completed. On a separate sheet of paper under each central idea you have chosen, write any secondary ideas you find. Your writing will form a simple outline of the major information in the reading.

    Example: Central idea:
                  Such undergraduate degree programs are
                  helping people like Peter get a college degree.

             Secondary ideas:
                  These degree programs are growing in
                  number.
                  Peter received a degree in business
                  administration.
                  Peter was the first son in his family to get a
                  college degree.

4. Action

Planning session scenario

The following is a role-play of six people at a planning session: two employees and two management representatives from a company and two college administrators. Divide the class into groups of about six or select six to present the meeting in front of the rest of the class.

The employees and company management want the college to begin a degree program at their facilities, but the college is not certain if it is a good idea. The employees and management must persuade the representatives from the college to try an in-house program. Listed below are important points each of the three parties should consider.

College administrators. What is the quality of students who will attend the program? Are they as good as the students who attend regular college classes? The college must maintain high standards.

Will the college lose money on the program? How long will the program continue? Administration costs are high, especially at first, when the programs must be organized.

What is the need for facilities such as libraries and laboratories? Without these facilities can the teacher teach and can the students study effectively?

They worry about changing the courses to meet the needs of the company employees. Will the quality of the courses be as high as the quality of the courses taught at the college campus?

Employees. The employees can't get a higher education without the in-house program.

The company will help pay the expenses, so this is a good opportunity for both the employees and the college.

The degree program will increase their chances for better jobs and higher pay in the future.

The employees do not want to study at regular colleges where the other students are younger than most of the employees.

Company management representatives. The management representatives think the program will raise the educational level of their employees.

Education will make the employees better supervisors.

Education will increase productivity.

An educational program will help in recruiting employees.

An educational program will help reduce employee turnover and will increase employee loyalty and morale.

5. Reaction

Questions for discussion

1. At colleges and universities, students study a wide range of courses while earning a degree. The courses offered at job sites, however, are sometimes tailored to a company's needs. Do you think the education offered at the job site may be more limited than the education offered at regular colleges? Can the same quality of education be provided at a company's facilities where there are no libraries or laboratories? Are there also possible educational advantages for an on-site degree program?

2. What is the attitude in your country about higher (beyond high school) education? Does your nation have similar programs which try to educate people who must work at a job? How do these programs differ from the programs discussed in the article?

3. Because of these job-site programs, the colleges which do the teaching receive tuition money; the students receive an education they might not have received otherwise; and the companies get better-educated and more loyal employees. Who benefits most from these degree programs?

RETAILING

CHAPTER FIVE: First-Class Secondhand Clothes

Patricia A. Dreyfus   *Money*

Secondhand* clothing is becoming popular. All over the U.S., shops that sell it report sales up by as much as 100% over the past two years. Much of the increase stems from a new sense of value. Says Marlene Bonk, owner of Mais Encore in Lake Forest, Ill.: "People will pay more today for used **better grade** clothing than for cheap, poorly made new merchandise."

To serious bargain hunters like Dorothy Neff of Ridgewood, N.J., the **merits*** of used clothing are **old hat.** Mrs. Neff, a professional singer and music teacher, discovered secondhand clothing stores 15 years ago. She started buying only evening wear for her concert performances, but before long most of the clothing she **acquired** for herself, her husband and two children was coming from **thrift shops.** "Al laughed at first, until I got him a Bill Blass jacket for $7."

Stores that sell secondhand clothes—as opposed to antique **apparel***, which can be very costly indeed—fall into two categories: resale stores and thrift shops. Resale stores are profit-making enterprises. They offer only clothing and **costume jewelry**, and **merchandise*** is sold **on consignment***, with half the selling price going to the item's original owner. Thrift shops are **nonprofit*** operations for the benefit of schools, hospitals and other **charities**. They depend on **donations*** for their stock, which is usually a **jumble** of clothing, furniture, jewelry, books, **bric-a-brac** and small appliances.

At resale stores, most merchandise is made up of unwanted **garments*** left off by individuals and is between one and three years old. But sometimes **department stores** and manufacturers use resale stores to **unload*** brand-new samples or excess **inventory***. Wherever it comes from, clothing is carefully examined for stains,

Secondhand: used, previously owned by someone else.
Better grade: higher quality.

Merits: advantages, good points.
Old hat: too well known, too common, old-fashioned (informal).
Acquired: got, obtained, bought.
Thrift shops: (see next paragraph of article).

Apparel: clothing.
Costume jewelry: inexpensive jewelry.
Merchandise: items for sale.
On consignment: with payment being made after merchandise has been sold by the receiver.
Nonprofit: not operated for personal financial benefit or advantage, as hospitals, churches, or certain clubs or organizations dedicated to the public good.
Charities: organizations which help needy people.
Donations: gifts.
Jumble: A disorganized mixture, variety.
Bric-a-brac: assorted, various items of little or no value.
Garments: pieces of clothing.
Department stores: large stores with a wide variety of merchandise.
To unload: to sell off at a low price or at a loss.
Inventory: selection of merchandise at any one time (in a store).

Retail price: price when the item reaches the public.
Wares: items for sale, merchandise.
Leftover: remaining, extra.

Decade: ten years.
Defects: faults, imperfections, something lacking in perfection.
Bins: large containers.
Catchall: here, accepting a variety of odds and ends.
Underpriced: priced lower than usual or too low.
Top: best.
Haggling: arguing over price.
Negotiable: which can be changed by argument or discussion.

Lines: series of goods put out by the same company.
Declined: became lower, decreased.
Reputation: public opinion of a person or thing.
Went for: sold for.

Bearing: carrying, having.

Tend to: are inclined to, are likely to.
Department: section.
Comparable: of similar quality or level.

Stock: supply of merchandise currently on hand.
Freshest: here, acquired recently.
To turn over: to exchange, to replace.
Wardrobes: personal stocks of clothes.
Prolific: very productive.
Heiress: woman who has inherited a large amount of money.

flaws and unfashionableness. As a rule, prices start at one-fourth to one-half of the original **retail price***. Most resale shops further reduce prices on unsold **wares** after a couple of months. Then **leftover** garments go back to the consignor or onto a sale table where they may sell for just a few dollars.

At thrift shops, quality is less certain. Clothes are from a few months to a **decade** old; though they require that goods be clean, charity shops will accept torn linings and other repairable **defects***. Prices are generally lower than in resale stores. Typically, there will be **bins*** of clothing marked $1 and $2. Cotton blouses on racks may cost $4 or $5; wool skirts might sell for $15. Because of thrift shops' **catchall*** policy, it takes more care to find good-quality, **underpriced** items, but such treasures do exist. A four-year-old Beged-Or suede coat that cost $350 new was recently priced at $38 at the Cancer Thrift Shop in New York; Encore, the city's **top** resale store, had an identical coat on sale for $110. And while **haggling*** only sometimes works in resale stores, prices in thrift shops are generally **negotiable***.

The biggest savings at secondhand stores are on famous name designer clothes. Usually, such garments were so expensive to begin with that prices have to be cut 75% or more the second time around. Although some designer **lines*** have **declined** in quality in recent years, often these clothes are good values at secondhand prices. At the Ritz Thrift Shop in New York, which is actually a resale store, a floor-length white coat by Galanos—one designer whose **reputation** has remained excellent—cost $3,450. No more than three years old, the garment originally **went for*** $25,000.

Many secondhand stores offer a wide selection of children's fashions. At Hand-Me-Downs, an Evanston, Ill., resale store, children's clothes **bearing*** labels ranging from Dior to Danskins cost $5 to $20.

Good buys in men's clothing are harder to find. "Men **tend to*** wear their clothes to death," explains Orest Kowaliv, co-owner of Exchange Unlimited, one of the few resale stores in New York that have a men's **department**. The store was recently selling a year-old Paul Stuart wool suit for $85; **comparable*** new suits cost $250. The Closet in Boston, also a resale store, sells only fine men's clothing. Prices are about one-third to one-half of what Saks and Lord & Taylor, located just across the street, charge for the same garments.

Stock is **freshest** in the more expensive resale shops, such as Encore Exchange in Brookline, Mass., and The Place in suburban Los Angeles, since wealthy women tend to **turn over** their more costly **wardrobes*** frequently. The most **prolific** consignor at Encore in New York is an oil **heiress** who spends close to $300,000 a year on clothes. So far this year she has sent in 463 garments, which originally cost from $60 to $3,500 each.

Thrift shops sponsor frequent sales and special events, where shoppers may find better-than-usual merchandise or lower-than-usual

A shopper examines an item at the Bargain Cupboard, a thrift shop on Long Island.

prices. In Boston, for example, Goodwill Industries sets aside a special room in its Berkeley Street store for a "Unique Boutique" every Tuesday. Most merchandise is **brand-new***, donated by local retailers. On one recent Tuesday, **bargain hunters** found $80 leather handbags on sale for $3 and $40 Gloria Vanderbilt jeans for $3.50.

Finding a good secondhand store can be as **challenging** as **sifting** through the merchandise once you're there. Looks are sometimes no clue to **value***. Mais Encore, in Lake Forest, Ill., is a steep climb up a narrow flight of stairs in a commercial building. Inside, however, five **cluttered** rooms bulge with clothing by Halston, Dior, Calvin Klein, and other designers. Stores operated by the Junior League in 111 cities are usually **a cut above** most charity shops. Other exceptionally well run thrift stores include the Blue Bird Circle in Houston, Trading Post in Lake Forest, and Girls Club or Spence-Chapin shops in New York.

Secondhand stores aren't for shoppers without time or **determination***. Buying used clothing is not always practical for women who work, since better thrift and resale shops tend to be located in residential neighborhoods, inconvenient for lunch-hour shopping. On Saturdays—the stores' busiest days—the selection is often **depleted***. Sizes on labels or **price tags*** may be **misleading***: secondhand clothes have frequently **shrunk*** or been **altered***. Mistakes are **irremediable**. Most shops have strict no-return, no-

Brand-new: completely new.
Bargain hunters: persons who shop for unusually low prices.

Challenging: difficult; fun because it is difficult.
Sifting: searching, looking carefully (through a great many things).
Value: amount of money something is worth; also, a good buy.
Cluttered: disorganized, jumbled, with many items not in their places.
A cut above: clearly better than (informal).

Determination: an attitude of not giving up, strength of purpose.
Depleted: exhausted, emptied, used up.
Price tags: small labels attached to the merchandise and bearing a price.
Misleading: giving a false impression, indicating the wrong idea.
Shrunk: become smaller, often as a result of washing (shrink, shrank, shrunk).
Altered: changed to fit better.
Irremediable: not correctable.

Chancy: risky, uncertain.
Getting stuck with: of merchandise, not being able to sell for a reasonable price.
Pelt: animal skin.

Subtler: less obvious, less visible.
Addiction: an unbreakable habit.
To accommodate: to make room for, to change for the purpose of reception.
Snob: person who is too proud or arrogant.

exchange policies. If a secondhand blouse does not match the outfit it was bought to go with, well, better luck next time.

Buying used furs is especially **chancy** because of the danger of **getting stuck with*** dried-out skins. A fur may look and feel fine, but if the **pelt** is dry it could split into ribbons after a few months' wear. Unless they really know how to distinguish the good from the bad, shoppers in the market for fur will probably do better at more expensive resale shops that want to protect their quality image.

While clothes that fall apart or colors that scream "mistake" as soon as you get them home are obviously hazards, there are **subtler*** dangers to buying secondhand clothes. "Thrift shops can become an **addiction**," says Dorothy Neff, who recently doubled her closet space to **accommodate*** her vast wardrobe. Judith Bobrosky, a weekly customer at Jean's Stars Apparel, a resale store in Sherman Oaks, Calif., agrees: "My biggest problem is that I buy too much because of the prices." Moreoever, adds Ms. Bobrosky, "I'm getting to be a **snob**. If something in my favorite thrift shop doesn't have a designer label, I won't buy it."

1. Business Vocabulary

A. Complete the sentences with appropriate forms of the words in parentheses.

1. (nonprofit, negotiable) Thrift shops are _____ stores, and sometimes the prices are _____ .
2. (haggle, defect, merchandise) If the shopper finds _____ in the _____ , she can _____ over the price.
3. (bin, value) If shoppers look carefully through the _____ in the stores, real _____ can be found.
4. (unload, bear) Department stores sometimes use resale stores to _____ excess merchandise which may _____ high-quality labels.
5. (price tag, retail price) The prices on the _____ are lower than what the _____ would be.
6. (inventory, go for, deplete) On busy days like Saturdays when shoppers really _____ low prices, a store's _____ may become _____ .
7. (secondhand, consignment) Much of the merchandise in resale shops is someone's _____ clothing which is sold on _____ .
8. (alter, shrink) Many of the items sold on consignment may not be the same size as is written on the label because they have _____ or have been _____ .
9. (garment, line) Many of the _____ found in these stores are from designer _____ .
10. (wardrobe, apparel) Some people fill their _____ with secondhand _____ .

B. Paraphrase each sentence below in a way that clearly shows the meaning of the word in italics. Do not use any form of the italicized word.

Example: Resale stores often sell clothing on *consignment*.

Solution: *Resale stores often sell clothing for other people and keep part of the profit.*

1. A *determined* shopper can frequently find values.
2. Some stores handle only *brand-new* merchandise, *donated* by retailers.
3. One person bought so much clothing that she had to expand her closet to *accommodate* her vast wardrobe.
4. One store was selling a good suit for $85; a *comparable* suit would cost $250 retail.
5. There are several *subtle* dangers in buying secondhand clothing.
6. The thrift stores frequently have a *catchall* policy.
7. Men's clothing *tends* to be harder to find.
8. Sizes written on labels can be *misleading*, and if the wrong size is bought, the mistake is irremediable.
9. When buying furs, it is especially easy *to get stuck with* a bad buy.
10. The *merits* of used clothing are well known.

2. Structural Review

Expressing action before an event in the past: past perfect tense.

Look at the following word pattern:

had + PAST PARTICIPLE

Sometimes there are two events which occur one after the other in the past.

Example: I wrote him; then he wrote me.

You may use the PAST PERFECT TENSE to express this relationship between the events.

Example: I *had written* him before he wrote me.

Example: He wrote me after I *had written* him.

The two events may not always be included within the same sentence.

Example: I saw John at the unemployment bureau. Perhaps he *had quit* his job.

When the time of the events is quite clear, the verbs can sometimes both be in the simple past.

Example: After I wrote him, he wrote me.

Replace the verb in parentheses with an appropriate form *using the past perfect form wherever possible*.

I (shop) _____ for secondhand clothes for about two months before my girlfriend (find out) _____. She laughed until one day I (buy) _____ her a pair of Calvin Klein jeans for $3.50. Then she (buy) _____ me a beautiful wool sweater that some department store (unload) _____. We (find) _____ a whole line of shoes that (be) _____ $90 a pair before prices were cut. Although the line (decline) _____ in quality in recent years, it (be) _____ still worth the thrift shop price.

Generally speaking, good used clothes (be) _____ impossible to find before the secondhand clothing boom (begin) _____. One particular pair of shoes (belong) _____ to an heiress.

I never (be) _____ a snob before I (begin) _____ shopping the thrift stores for used clothes.

3. Business Communications

Note taking: Recognizing unnecessary information

To take accurate notes, you must be able to find the central idea, find the secondary information, and recognize the unnecessary information. Not all information is important.

In the groups of sentences given below, choose the sentences you think include the central idea and the secondary ideas. Eliminate the unnecessary information.

1. a. Sales of secondhand clothing are up 100% over the past two years.
   b. People will pay more for used, better-grade clothing than for poorly made new clothing.
   c. Secondhand clothing is becoming popular.
   d. Most resale stores have garments that were unwanted.
   e. Most merchandise in resale stores is between one and three years old.

2. a. Department stores and manufacturers use resale stores to unload merchandise.
   b. At resale stores, the merchandise is better than the merchandise at thrift stores.
   c. Sometimes resale stores have brand-new merchandise.
   d. Prices are usually one-fourth to one-half the original retail price.
   e. Unsold garments go back to the consignor.

3. a. Many stores offer a wide selection of children's fashions.
   b. Designer prices are so high to begin with, that they have to be reduced by 75% or more at a secondhand store.
   c. Although some designer lines have declined in quality, these clothes are often good values at secondhand prices.
   d. The biggest savings at secondhand stores are on designer clothes.
   e. Good buys in men's clothing are hard to find.

4. a. There are subtle dangers in buying secondhand clothing.
   b. Some secondhand clothing may be smaller than what is written on the label because some garments shrink or may have been altered.
   c. Stock is freshest at the more expensive resale shops.
   d. Buying secondhand clothing requires determination.
   e. Shopping for secondhand clothes may become an addiction.

4. Action

Interview with a loan officer

Divide the class into groups of two or three. One person (or two persons forming a partnership) wants to begin a business in clothing resale, but does not have enough capital.

Conduct an interview between the loan officer and the person(s) applying for the loan. The officer must become convinced that the resale clothing business is profitable. Consider the following points:

Business person(s) Explain that the business is to be a resale shop, not a thrift shop.
   Explain the difference between the two kinds of shops.
   Know whether or not the store will handle designer clothing or furs in addition to regular clothing.
   Know what the monthly costs will be, such as rent, merchandise, salaries.
   Have an idea how much money can be made monthly.
   Know how much money you want to borrow.

Loan officer Find out the exact nature of the business.
Find out how other resale shops in the nation are prospering.
Find out where the business person will get the merchandise.
Find out how quickly the merchandise will sell so that the old merchandise will not remain in the store for several months.
Find out how large the market is for used clothing.
Find out how prices will be determined.
Find out if the business person will handle ordinary clothing, designer clothing, or furs.
Find out how quickly the loan can be repaid.

5. Reaction

Questions for discussion

1. Do resale stores sound like good businesses to go into? Some of the more expensive garments like designer clothing must be reduced by as much as 75%. Can a profit be made? Also, isn't old clothing more difficult to sell than new clothing?
2. Is this done only in the United States? Is this done in other countries? Why are resale and thrift stores so common in America?
3. Resale stores are a new development. Why have they been created? Is the reason related to the general strength or weakness of the economy and the rate of inflation?
4. Do you think these stores will be able to sell enough clothing and attract enough customers to become a challenge to clothing retailers? The article mentioned that some people buy almost all of their clothing at these stores. Will enough people do this that retailers will suffer?

CHAPTER SIX: **Retailing Without Stores**

Larry J. Rosenberg and
Elizabeth C. Hirschman

Harvard Business Review

*Will stores become **extinct** in American retailing? This article argues that the answer is yes—or, at least, yes for great areas of retailing. **Telecommunication** will make it possible to order merchandise from the home; delivery systems will take the place of pickups by customers; banks and other financial organizations will handle money transfers. But technological possibility is only part of the story. Growing numbers of Americans appear to be interested in the time-saving convenience and breadth of choice that can be offered by telecommunication shopping, to say nothing of the fuel economies that would be possible.*

Extinct: no longer in existence.
Telecommunication: electronic communication (often, "telecommunications").

A revolution is under way in the store-**dominated** world of retailing. The **instigators** are nonstore **retailers*** who are appearing in new forms, proliferating in numbers, and gaining **market* share** from store-based retailers. Although accurate sales figures for this non-store growth are hard to **come by**, one source estimates that nonstore annual sales are **expanding*** from three to five times faster than those of traditional store **outlets***.[1] Here are some examples of the rise of nonstore retailing:

Dominated: controlled.
Instigators: people who initiate or start something.
Retailers: the merchants who offer merchandise to the public.
Market: place where people meet to buy and sell goods; the entirety of all possible business (for an item).
Market share: all the proportion that any one company has of all the business being done with respect to one kind of goods or services.
To come by: to obtain, get.
Expanding: growing larger, increasing in size.
Outlets: retail establishments, places of business for public buying.
Generated: created, occasioned, caused by.

- The increasing volume of telephone- and mail-**generated*** orders received by traditional store retailers such as Bloomingdale's, J.C. Penney, and Sears, Roebuck & Co.
- The increased popularity of in-flight shopping catalogs of major airline companies.

[1] William R. Davidson and Alice Rodgers, "Nonstore Retailing: Its Importance to and Impact on Merchandise Suppliers," *The Growth of Nonstore Retailing* (New York: New York University, Institute of Retail Management, 1979).

• The expanding selection of merchandise offerings made to credit customers by VISA, MasterCard, and American Express.

We expect this trend toward nonstore retailing to accelerate rapidly with the development of telecommunication retail systems. A description of how such a system may work is depicted in *Exhibit I*.

Consumers* with accounts at the telecommunication merchandiser will shop at home for a variety of products and services. Using an in-home **video display** catalog, they will order products from a participating retailer. When the order is received on its computer, this retailer will **assemble*** the goods from a fully **automated warehouse***. Simultaneously, **funds*** will be transferred from the customer's to the retailer's bank account. Customers will choose between picking up the order at a nearby distribution point or having it delivered to their door. There will be no fee for picking up the order. However, there may be a delivery charge of approximately $5. The charge will depend on the amount of the order and delivery time requirements (whether the next day at the company's convenience or at a confirmed time when the customer is at home).

We expect consumers to choose from among many kinds of retail combinations, with some continuing to shop mostly at stores, some using both mail order and stores, some combining telecommunication shopping and store shopping, and some shopping almost exclusively by telecommunication systems. Most people will move steadily toward telecommunication shopping, though the other types of shopping will never completely disappear.

Seeds of change

When consumers and the technology are ready, the experts agree, entrepreneurs will launch telecommunication merchandising in various cities across the nation. The readiness of consumers is a key* question. Will enough of them ever desire this new shopping experience and accept the **novel*** technology that such systems involve? Actually, there is evidence already that a sufficient number of consumers are emerging to support telecommunication merchandising. Developments like the following are relevant:

• A higher proportion of women are entering the **work force** (they have less time to shop).

• Desire for increased leisure time to **further** self-development and creative expression (means less time to go from store to store).

• Heightened consumer demand for specialty products and services (they are often hard to get in most shopping centers).

Each of these trends indicates consumers' willingness to change. They will be attracted by the greater diversity of merchandise than shopping centers can offer, as well as the smaller investment of time required.

Consumers: buyers, shoppers, customers.
Video: visual; often, using a TV screen.
Display: something presented for viewing; or often made visible for selection by shoppers.
Assemble: put together, fit together.
Automated: operating without human control.
Warehouse: a large building for storage.
Funds: money, often for a specific purpose.

Novel: new or strange, not previously known.

Work force: all the workers available to an industry or nation.

To further: to increase, to encourage.

Exhibit I
"Shopping" at home

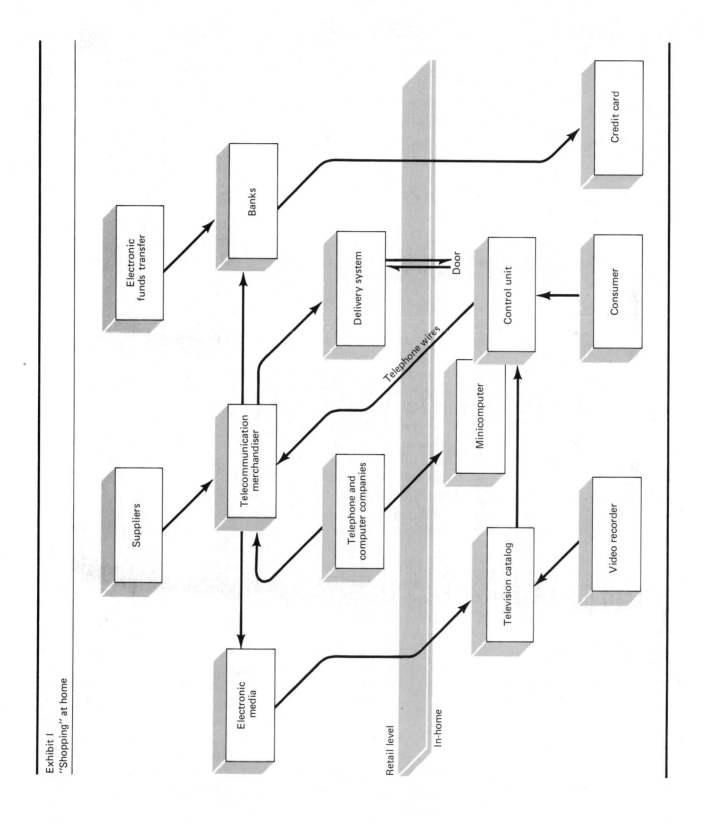

Conceptual leap

Enabling: making possible.
Conventional: traditional, most frequently occurring.

Telecommunication shopping is more than technological equipment **enabling** changes in buying habits. It represents a great leap beyond the **conventional*** concept of retailing.

This new system of retailing we will call an *offering system*, since it will make a total product-service offering available to subscribing customers. It will have four unique features:

1. A variety of businesses, performing the functions of production, data exchange, warehousing, communications, and payment, will be involved, simultaneously rather than **sequentially**.

Sequentially: one after the other.

2. Distribution systems will become diversified and more competitive.

3. Financial systems will become heavily involved in retailing in order to create various payment arrangements.

4. Consumers will be actively involved in the system, somewhat like members of a large **co-op**.

Co-op (cooperative): a business completely owned and operated by those using the services.

Responses of retailers

What do retail executives think about the future of telecommunication shopping and offering systems? We have discussed the possibilities with a number of executives, often asking for their reactions to the various scenarios possible. Their opinions range from extreme **skepticism** to **confident*** belief.

Skepticism: strong doubt.
Confident: certain.

Some executives doubt the **viability** of telecommunication assistance in retail **transactions***. One manager of a major national retail chain told us: "It seems that every ten years the 'experts' **forecast** the **advent*** of electronic in-home ordering which is 'sure' to come during the next ten years. It has not happened yet, and frankly, we don't see it happening anytime soon. Those who prefer to shop at home can use our catalog instead of their television set."

Viability: practicality.
Transactions: business deals, acts of buying or selling.
Forecast: predict, foretell.
Advent: beginning, initiation, start.

To be sure, a substantial proportion of consumers are using catalogs for retail purchasing assistance. For example, in 1977, 9.1% of Sears, Roebuck's business originated from its catalogs, with 11.4% of sales coming from catalog counters in Sears stores, making a total of about 20% for catalog-generated sales. This sales proportion has remained constant at Sears for the past five years.

A contrasting perspective is the belief of some retailers that telecommunication retailing will **complement***, but not replace, existing forms of nonstore retailing, such as catalog, door-to-door, and direct-mail selling. An executive **affiliated*** with a communication corporation asserted: "We see telecommunication as one important way to extend retailers' contacts with consumers. It can supplement their traditional **promotion** and distribution tools. Some retailers will find it of more use than others, depending on who their customers are and what products they are selling."

Complement: to go together well with, to complete.
Affiliated: associated (with an organization or institution) either formally or informally.
Promotion: advertising or publicity.

Although industry executives differ in their opinions of the applicability of telecommunication to their own retailing operations, most tell us they do not **rule** it **out** and state that **alternative** systems are under study. One manager of a specialty chain summed up this view: "Yes, we are actively considering telecommunication systems. We make every attempt to **keep abreast** of technological developments which may affect our business. One major factor in any decision we might reach concerning telecommunication would, of course, be competitors' use of it. We don't want to be the last to implement it."

Rule out: say there is no possibility.
Alternative: other, substitute.
To keep abreast: to keep up with, to stay informed about.

Will retailing be transformed?

What will be the specific effects on traditional retailing brought about by the emergence of offering systems? We foresee many important changes. It seems likely that traditional retailers will become increasingly **vulnerable** as telecommunication shopping **catches on**.

Vulnerable: able to be attacked, defenseless.
Catches on: becomes popular.

First, as consumers desire more uniqueness and individuality, fewer and fewer products will be purchased without regard to style, fashion, or social meaning. The present movement into apparel by discount and mass-merchandise stores may be partially **stymied*** by the consumer's desire to buy something that no one else has. The atmosphere and **assortment** in discount and mass-merchandise stores will fall far short of the individuality that consumers increasingly will demand. Small local stores will be at a disadvantage to diversify and individualize their **merchandise mix***.

Stymied: stopped completely, obstructed or stopped movement of.
Assortment: variety, selection, choice.
Merchandise mix: selection of things for sale.

Second, the movement toward in-home purchasing will hurt traditional retailers. Those retailers who refuse or are slow to develop to-the-home approaches will inevitably suffer.

Third, as consumers become more **discerning** and produce a higher rate of **product returns***, repairs, and exchanges, many retailers will feel greater pressure on profit margins. Many retail enterprises require high sales volume to offset low prices. Increased product returns will lower **net** volume and push up **operating costs***. While it is doubtful, for example, that many department stores will **fold*** because of increasing product returns, it is likely that their profitability will be reduced. This should be a greater problem for smaller retailers.

Discerning: able to make good decisions, insightful, perceptive.
Product returns: bringing back an item to the seller because it is defective or unsatisfactory.
Net: remaining after all necessary deductions or all losses.
Operating costs: expenses necessary to run a business.
Fold: here, go out of business, close permanently because of financial difficulties.

Fourth, the key conditions underlying traditional retailing seem to be changing. Many store-based companies depend on a steady stream of automobile-driving consumers who visit an outlet, select a product, and take it home. A decrease in each of these habits seriously threatens the retailer's competitive health. Consumers are more reluctant to spend time inefficiently searching for products among the long, crowded aisles typical of many stores, when instead they can order many of the same products from a catalog or by telephone.

Energy shortages and costs, especially for gasoline, will serve to reduce further the willingness and ability of consumers to shop as they traditionally have. Frequent trips to a store to buy a few items will be sharply **curtailed**. Major shopping trips will be more

Curtailed: reduced, decreased.

carefully planned. The in-home use of electronic catalogs becomes an increasingly valuable and desirable shopping alternative.

Conclusion

Virtual: practical, essential.
Era: a relatively long period of time.
Post-revolution: after the revolution (mentioned at the beginning of the article).

We see as a **virtual*** certainty that the **era** of widespread telecommunication shopping is approaching. We predict that this era will see significant alterations in the concept of retailing and the nature of retail competition. Like all predictions of great change, this forecast is uncertain. However, it is worth stressing that our picture of the **post-revolution** retailing scene is based partly on information available today, as well as our reasoned opinion of probable outcomes.

To unfold: here, to become visible.
Formulating: inventing, making a formula for.

Corporations involved in any way with retailing cannot afford to ignore the developments described. Nor can executives of store-based retailers, shopping center developers, brand-name manufacturers, broadcasters, computer manufacturers, telecommunication suppliers, banks, and credit-card companies wait for the future to **unfold** before **formulating** appropriate strategies. The challenge to management in all these retail-related industries is to understand the dimensions of the coming telecommunication revolution. Soon it will be time to participate in that revolution.

1. Business Vocabulary

A. From the list of words provided, fill in the blanks in the following memorandum. Each word is to be used only one time.

transactions   merchandise mix
retailing   market
operating   funds
product returns   outlets
retailer   assemble
warehouses   consumers
expanding   confident

MEMORANDUM

Date: January 23, 19—
To: Deborah Boyles
From: Rod Sprague
Subject: Telecommunications in retailing

Deborah, I want some information on the use of telecommunications in the _____ business. Our job is to sell more merchandise and increase our _____ share. In the past we have done this by increasing the number of our store _____ and by _____ our sales volume.

However, in the future _____ will be shopping at home with a video display catalog which will be provided by a participating _____. Automated _____ will _____ the goods and banks will transfer _____ to pay for the merchandise.

I am _____ that these sorts of _____ will increase. We must prepare an effective promotion for our goods and we must keep a broad _____.

Could you please study any possible problems such as _____ which might lower our profit margin? Also investigate all _____ costs.

B. Next to each sentence, write the letter of the words which are *closest in meaning* to the underlined word in that sentence.

A. stopped completely, frustrated
B. everyday, normal
C. extremely important
D. connected with, belonging to
E. beginning
F. very new
G. make complete, perfect
H. created by the mail
I. practically
J. collapse

_____ 1. It is *virtually* certain that telecommunications systems will become a part of retailing.

_____ 2. The readiness of consumers is a *key* question.

_____ 3. Will the public accept the *novel* technology of such systems?

_____ 4. Telecommunications represent an advance beyond the *conventional* understanding of retailing.

_____ 5. The *advent* of in-home ordering has been mentioned before by experts.

_____ 6. Some people say that telecommunications will *complement* rather than replace present forms of retailing.

_____ 7. The article mentions one executive *affiliated* with a communications corporation.

_____ 8. It is doubtful that department stores will *fold* because of the new systems.

_____ 9. When the consumers' desires are greatly different from a retailer's plans, the retailer may be *stymied*.

_____ 10. Stores like J.C. Penney and Bloomingdale's are receiving many *mail-generated* orders.

2. Structural Review

Expressing limited duration: The progressive tenses

The progressive tenses are used to express an action lasting for a limited time or an event in process. Continuation is emphasized. The progressive forms may appear in any of the English tenses. In this chapter's article, uses of the progressive are limited to the present and the future because of the subject matter. Other tenses of the progressive will be dealt with in later chapters.

To express duration of an event or action in the present tense, use:

is/are + VB + *-ing*

Present tense example: Merchants *are increasing* retail sales by using catalogs. (This is not an eternal truth, but is true in the present for a time limited for several reasons.)

To express duration of an event or action in the future use:

will + *be* + VB + *-ing*

Future tense example: More women *will be entering* the work force. (Again, this was not true formerly and will not always be true, but will continue to be true for a limited time in the future.)

The following short discourse requires the future and present progressive tenses. Supply the correct verb form in the appropriate progressive tense.

A revolution is under way across the nation. Today, nonstore retailers (appear) _____ in new forms and (proliferate) _____ in large numbers. They (gain) _____ market share from store-based retailers. One estimate is that next year nonstore annual sales (expand) _____ five times as fast as those of traditional outlets. We expect that this trend toward nonstore retailing (accelerate) _____ rapidly with the development of telecommunication retail systems. A higher proportion of women (enter) _____ the work force and will have less time to shop.

Already consumers (demand) _____ specialty products and services which are often hard to get in most shopping centers. In short, there are multiple reasons why entrepreneurs across the nation soon (launch) _____ telecommunication merchandising.

3. Business Communications

Memoranda

A memorandum (or memo) is a type of business letter. It is informal and is usually sent and used only within an office or department. The memorandum is frequently more personal than a business letter because of its informality. The language used is often like spoken English.

The information required at the beginning of the memorandum is (1) Date, (2) To, (3) From, and (4) Subject. These words (or words with the same meanings) are printed on special stationery for memos. "Memo" or "Memorandum" is printed at the top of the page. Memoranda* usually end with nothing more than the writer's signature. Neither a formal opening nor a formal close is used.

Since memoranda are written primarily to communicate information, the style of writing is usually direct and factual. Study the following as an example of format and writing style.

---

*The formal plural of memorandum is *memoranda*, although in many business communications the word *memorandums* occurs.

MEMORANDUM

Date: June 13, 19—
To: David Sonenschein
From: Bobby Tanimoto
Subject: Retailing trends

David, I am concerned about our company and the future of retailing. Americans are becoming more and more interested in time-saving shopping conveniences and in variety of merchandise. We presently offer ordering services by catalog and by telephone. In the future, however, telecommunications offerings will be increasing.

Can you please investigate this area of telecommunications in retailing and report back to me by the end of the month on what you find? We must stay well-informed.

Now write a memorandum for each of the following situations.

1. You are A. L. Riggs. You work for a construction company. Your company is going to build a new shopping center beside a creek. You want Mr. Jack Mc-Connell, your employee, to study the possible effect this may have on the creek's ecology. You anticipate that the citizens of the town will be concerned about the creek, and you want to study the situation in order to avoid problems.

2. The mail department in your company has been slow in performing its duties recently. Both outgoing and incoming mail have not been moving as rapidly as they should, and some mistakes in sorting have occurred. You want Mr. Mc-Connell to observe the mailroom operations and work with the head of the mailroom to solve problems.

3. Put yourself in the place of the subordinate writing a memo to his superior. You are now Mr. Jack McConnell, and you are to respond to your superior, A. L. Riggs, concerning the requests made above.

4. Action

Scenario for a personnel meeting

Your company has weekly personnel meetings, and this week's objective is to exchange information about the future of retailing systems.

Form class members into small groups. Each member of the group is to take one part of the article and make notes on that part and write the notes in summary form. After all members of the group have completed their summaries, each person is to present his summary orally, keeping to the order of the ideas in the article.

5. Reaction

Questions for discussion

1. Is this article limited in scope to the United States? The credit cards VISA, American Express, and MasterCard are American, as are the department stores mentioned. Will telecommunications retailing systems be used in other nations? When?

2. Many people already use small computers in their homes. How might this encourage the use of telecommunications sooner? Will it be in this century? Will it be limited only to a few wealthy people?

3. The article speaks of the "consumer's willingness to change." Do you think consumers really want to change to a system by which they no longer go to the stores for shopping? Would many people want to give up the opportunity for window shopping in stores? Will the general public want to change?

ECONOMICS

CHAPTER SEVEN: The Free Market Incentive: Self-Interest vs. Greed

E. Woodrow Eckard, Jr.   *Business Economics*

Vs.: against.

Zero-sum game: a situation in which if one person wins, another must lose, rather than a situation in which both can gain at the same time.
Drag: anything which slows something down.

Commonplace: common.
Impetus: this article deals with human motivation—the reasons for human actions. Several words with similar or related meanings are used in order to avoid repetition: *motivation, motive, motive force, driving force, impetus, dynamic,* and *incentive*. By paying attention to the contexts of these words, try to see how they differ in meaning.
Free enterprise: conducting industry and trade with the minimum of government control.
Capitalistic: pertaining to the economy in which a country's trade and industry are organized and controlled by the owners of capital.
Profit motive: reason for doing things in order to gain personal wealth.
Greed: selfish desire to improve one's own situation *at the expense of others*.
Considered: here, of the opinion, regarded as, thought of as.
Synonymous: meaning the same thing.
Presumption: assumption, supposition, guess.
Connotations: meanings (of a word) beyond the fundamental meaning.
Objectionable: displeasing, unsatisfactory.
Compounded: here, increased greatly.
Laissez-faire: allowing individual activities to be conducted without government control.

The idea that the effectiveness of capitalist economic systems arises from the greedy behavior of individuals comes in part from misunderstandings of Adam Smith's famous statements regarding self-interest. In fact, Smith did not feel self-interest and selfishness were equal. He was referring instead to "the natural effort of every individual to better his own condition." However, a more basic problem is that the idea of a greed-driven economy suggests a **zero-sum game** *in which one person's gain can be obtained only at the expense of others. This goes against the realities of a free enterprise economy in which exchange cannot usually occur unless it is mutually beneficial. Greedy behavior, or cheating, actually is a* **drag** *on the system. The net effect of this misunderstanding has been to create unwarranted suspicions of economic activity and to produce a systematic bias toward over-regulation.*

It is **commonplace** today to hear that the **impetus** behind **free-enterprise***, **capitalistic*** economic systems is the selfish behavior of individuals. The **profit motive*** and "greed" are almost universally **considered*** synonymous. This **presumption***, with its clearly implied negative moral **connotations***, creates an **objectionable*** image of free-enterprise economic activity. The problem is **compounded** by the common tendency to attribute this belief to Adam Smith, the "father" of **laissez-faire*** economic theory. In fact, Smith's well-known statements regarding self-interest are often quoted as "proof" that it is indeed selfishness which provides the driving force in a free market economy.

The author acknowledges helpful comments from N. R. Borofsky, G. E. Briefs, T. G. Marx, and T. F. Walton. Any remaining errors, and all opinions expressed herein, are the sole responsibility of the author.

The purpose of this paper is to point out, first, that Smith's concept of self-interest has been seriously misinterpreted. He had in mind something much different than narrow selfishness. Second, and perhaps more fundamentally, it is shown that under a **regime** of free exchange, opportunities to behave selfishly are actually reduced. Finally, it is argued that this confusion regarding the motive economic force underlies much of **public policy** regarding **private sector*** economic activity, particularly the increasingly apparent tendency toward over-regulation.

Regime: rule, reign.
Public policy: governmental regulation.
Private sector: the area of economy having to do with individuals and companies controlled by individuals (nongovernmental).

Smith's concept of self-interest

The association of selfishness with Smith's theory is, no doubt, due to his reliance on individual self-interest as the behavioral cornerstone of his theoretical structure. He did, in the *Wealth of Nations*, often **explicitly** identify self-interest as the prime motive force underlying a free economy.

Explicitly: specifically, exactly.

However, Smith's references to self-interest have been misinterpreted. In particular, it is common to **characterize*** the behavior thus implied in a **pejorative** manner, i.e., as being "selfish."

To characterize: to describe, to attribute certain qualities to.
Pejorative: speaking badly of or expressing a low opinion about.

The problem with these characterizations is simply that they pervert Smith's original meaning. Terms such as "selfish" or "greedy" both denote and connote morally objectionable behavior. But, as noted by E. G. West, Smith had something entirely different in mind.

> . . . 'self-love' in Smith's philosophy is, in its proper setting, one of the human **virtues**. It is certainly not to be confused with selfishness.[1]

Virtues: any good human qualities or characteristics, such as honor, justice, or courage.

An alternative statement by Smith of the source and effect of the basic economic force makes this point clear:

> The natural effort of every individual to better his own condition, when suffered to exert itself with freedom and security, is so powerful a principle, that it is alone, and without any assistance, . . . capable of carrying on the society to wealth and prosperity. . . .[2]

Thus, by individual self-interest, Smith is referring to "the natural effort of every individual to better his own condition. . . ." This concept of self-interest is much more general in scope than selfishness alone. While selfish behavior is one means by which an individual can "better his own condition," experience suggests that it is in fact but a small **subset** of all self-interested behavior.

Subset: a set within a set or a group within a group.

It seems **cynical** indeed to characterize these underlying "self-interested motives" as selfish. In fact, the simple desire to better one's life could be claimed as the motive underlying *all* forms of human effort; e.g., in the arts and science, as well as in the economic **sphere**.

Cynical: distrustful of motives of others.
Sphere: here, area, field, or domain.

[1] E. G. West, in the introduction to *The Theory of Moral Sentiments* by Adam Smith, Liberty Classics: Indianapolis, 1976 (originally published in 1759), at 27.
[2] A. Smith, *The Wealth of Nations*, The University of Chicago Press: Chicago, 1976 (originally published in 1776), vol. 2, at 49–50.

Insight: understanding.
Benevolence: the doing of good for others.
Perforce: necessarily.

In short, Smith did not consider greed to be the motive force underlying the success of capitalism. His great **insight**, as suggested by R. H. Coase, was simply that the success of a free enterprise economic system does not depend on universal **benevolence**.[3] This is particularly important in modern economies where each of us relies on the cooperation of large numbers of unknown individuals—individuals with whom, **perforce**, we can develop no feelings of mutual benevolence. Therefore, an economic system which relies on the existence of such feelings would be ineffectual indeed. In Smith's words:

Brethren: brothers or members of same group (rarely used today).
To prevail: to succeed.
Brewer: one who makes beer.

> . . . man has almost constant occasion for the help of his **brethren**, and it is in vain for him to expect it from their benevolence only. He will be more likely to **prevail** if he can interest their self-love in his favor, and show them that it is for their own advantage to do for him what he requires of them. . . . It is not from the benevolence of the butcher, the **brewer**, or the baker, that we expect our dinner, but from their regard to their own interest.[4]

Lot: here, situation, fate, luck.

In other words, the nearly universal personal desire to simply improve one's **lot** in life can be relied upon to provide the individual motivation* necessary for the system to work.

Selfishness and the free market system

Indifferent: not caring.

However, aside from confusions in interpreting Smith, a more fundamental problem exists. The use of such words as "selfishness" or "greed" to describe the motive force in an economic system carries with it the suggestion that the system is, in effect, a "zero-sum game"—i.e., one person's gain (i.e., "profit") is necessarily another's loss. Within such a system, the dynamic must be supplied by people **indifferent** to the losses imposed on others by activity designed to create gain for themselves, i.e., people whose behavior could reasonably be described as selfish.

Induce: persuade, convince.

But a free enterprise economic system is not a zero-sum game. Anyone can simply refuse to participate in a transaction which results in a net personal loss of welfare. One person can **induce** another to engage in an exchange *only* by offering terms which the second person perceives as improving his own welfare. Thus the dynamic in this system is provided by individuals who seek gain for themselves by offering gain to others. Each person's gain occurs, not at the expense of others, but instead in conjunction with the betterment of others. It seems of little use to characterize mutually beneficial (i.e., profitable) behavior of this type as "selfishness" on the part of either party involved.

Opportunistic: preferring what can be done to what should be done. Often there is a connotation of immorality or selfishness.

Nevertheless, in a world in which accurate information is costly to obtain, **opportunistic*** trading behavior can occur. However, since

---

[3] R. H. Coase, "The Wealth of Nations," *Economic Inquiry*, Vol. XV, No. 3 (July 1977), at 314–15.
[4] A. Smith, *The Wealth of Nations*, supra note 2, Vol. 1, at 18.

such behavior will be discovered after the trade, the **perpetrator**'s future sales will be **adversely** affected. Initial customers, once "**burned**," are not likely to return, and, as knowledge of this behavior spreads, potential new customers are made **wary**. Thus, the threat of reduced future sales becomes a serious **deterrent** to those individuals who might otherwise tend to cheat.

This built-in security against "greedy" behavior is particularly strong in modern manufacturing industries characterized by the existence of long-lived specialized assets. In these industries large initial investments are required for the construction or purchase of **assets*** (e.g., plant and machinery). Therefore, the value of a manufacturing firm depends on sales anticipated to occur many years in the future. If the firm acts initially so as to greatly reduce the likelihood of realizing such sales (e.g., through misrepresenting product quality), its value is reduced; and its owners thereby suffer a significant loss of wealth. In effect, manufacturers **guarantee*** the quality of their products by offering the value of their assets as "hostage" to consumers who can punish opportunistic behavior by simply withholding future purchases.

Conclusions

In summary, the common **assertion*** that greed is the necessary driving force behind a free-enterprise economic system is a **gross** distortion of reality. The implications of this confusion for national economic policy are significant. First, in an environment in which greed is seen as the prime moving force behind economic activity, success in such activity can be misinterpreted as *prima facie* evidence of wrongdoing (i.e., selfish or greedy behavior). For example, **antitrust** authorities tend to view high profits as evidence of monopoly power, not efficiency. Economic policy derived from such perceptions can serve only to undermine the incentive system on which the **efficacy** of free markets is based.

Furthermore, policy based on the notion that greedy behavior **abounds** in a free market is certain to result in a substantial over-**commitment** of resources to policing the system. It is becoming increasingly clear that such government-imposed **restraints*** on trade are becoming a major drag on the American economy. This state of affairs is not likely to change until fundamental and deeply **ingrained** perceptions of the motive force driving the free-market economic system are *radically* altered.

Perpetrator: one who commits an unfair act.
Adversely: negatively, disadvantageously, for the worse.
Burned: hurt by unfair business practice.
Wary: not trusting, on guard.
Deterrent: anything that might prevent or discourage an action (such as cheating).

Assets: anything owned that is worth money and may be sold to pay debts.
Guarantee: Offer assurance that something will be done or that something is true.

Assertion: statement, affirmation.
Gross: great, massive.
Prima facie: at first view or sight, from the most obvious point of view.
Antitrust: for the purpose of regulating monopoly.
Efficacy: effectiveness, power to produce effects or get results.

Abounds: is plentiful.
Commitment: something which one has promised, a pledge.
Restraints: restrictions, something that prevents or holds back.
Ingrained: deeply rooted.
Radically: very basically, drastically.

1. Business Vocabulary

A. A letter of transmittal accompanies a report being sent from one person to another, and introduces the report to the receiver, explaining its purpose and content.

Look at the letter of transmittal below. Fill in the blanks with a correct form of one of the words in the list provided. Each word is to be used only once.

opportunistic   presumption
consider   motivation
assertion   guarantee
restraint   objectionable

March 15, 198–

1503 S. Drake St.
Seattle, WA 72103

Professor Daryl Smith
Department of Business
Cypress College
Oakmont, NY 10078

Dear Professor Smith:

Enclosed you will find an article which agrees with my report. This article, like my report, disagrees with the _____ that greed is the driving force behind free enterprise.

The author of the article suggests that _____ for work comes from the personal desire to improve one's lot in life. In spite of this, many people _____ greed and the profit motive to mean the same. Of course, this is a _____ which creates an _____ image of free-enterprise economic activities. People must understand, though, that in a capitalistic economic system, _____ behavior will be punished by the consumer. In fact, manufacturers _____ the quality of their products by offering the value of their assets as "hostages" to consumers who can punish this sort of behavior. Lastly, the public does not know that the free market is policed by governmental _____ on trade.

I trust the article and this letter will serve as an adequate introduction to my enclosed report.

Respectfully yours,

Charles P. Foreman

B. Complete the following sentences with an appropriate form of the word in parentheses.

  1. (presume)   The author states that there is a common _____ that self-interest and greed are the same.
                  We should not _____ this to be true without first studying the subject, he says.

  2. (connote)   The term "self-interest" in free enterprise economics has taken on negative _____.
                  Objectionable behavior is _____ by terms such as "selfish" or "greedy."

  3. (capital)   Plant and machinery represent _____ investments.
                  A_____ society operates in a free-market economic system.
                  _____ is not, says Smith, motivated by greed.

  4. (character) The author objects to the _____ of economic self-interest as greedy behavior.
                  He says it is not helpful to _____ profitable behavior as selfish behavior.

C. Choose a word from the list below that fits each definition.

  assets   profit motive
  private sector   laissez-faire
  free enterprise

    Example: An investor of capital in business
                Answer: A capitalist

  1. the doctrine that government should not interfere with commerce
  2. the freedom of private business to operate competitively for profit
  3. items owned by a person or business together considered as components of wealth
  4. industries or activities within the domain of the free enterprise system
  5. the driving force in a private enterprise economic system

2. Structural Review

Past but continuing action: Present perfect progressive

The progressive tense (see also Chapter Six) also occurs in combination with the present perfect tense (see also Chapter Four). It indicates an action or state which began in the past but which *still continues*.

    Example: The author says that many people *have been presuming* that the free enterprise system is a zero-sum game.
                (They began assuming it in the past and *continue to assume it*.)

Example: Opportunistic trading behavior *has been occurring* since long before Adam Smith. (It began long ago *and still continues*.)

The present perfect progressive tense is used very frequently, but it is *almost never obligatory*. In the following paragraph, consider the verbs which are underlined and decide which *you* would write in the present perfect progressive tense, to emphasize that the action began in the past and its continuation in the present. Bring your own paragraph to class and discuss which verbs you have written in the present perfect progressive and give your reasons for doing so.

In this chapter, the author has written an article making a distinction between "greed" and "self-interest" in the free-market system. He says that for some time critics have complained that the motive force behind capitalism is simple greed. At the same time, other economists have proposed that the dynamic of capitalism is, in fact, nothing but cheating. They claim that the motive force of the U.S. economy is greed and insist that Adam Smith himself considered capitalism to be based on selfishness. Smith stated that the fundamental motivation in the free market system is self-interest.

The author of the article is suggesting that for some time these critics have confused Smith's broad concept of self-interest with a narrower idea of selfishness. He continues by defending the present economic system in general against the attacks which critics make. However, since his article a number of sociologists have continued their criticisms and have received attention from liberal groups. Although recently many thinkers are attempting to resolve the issue, an early solution does not appear likely.

3. Business Communications

A.   Using graphs

Graphs often accompany an article to clarify and aid the reader with particularly detailed information. (See the graphs in Chapters Ten, Eleven, and Fourteen.) Graphs can be used to display various points in an article, or to pinpoint very specific information. They are also extremely useful in presenting information that is difficult to explain in reading, such as changes in amounts or figures over a period of time. The visual picture helps the reader understand the information easily and quickly. They always contain quantitative data.

The ability to interpret graphs and convey the information contained in them orally can be very helpful to people in business. Graphs provide visual aids for oral presentations to be used at conferences, sales meetings, board meetings, and managerial meetings. They help keep the listeners interested and involved, and provide a different means—a visual one—of conveying information that might otherwise be too difficult for the listener to conceptualize.

There are many different types of graphs. The three most frequently used in business, however, are the *bar graph*, the *line graph*, and the *circle graph*. The use of these three types of graphs is discussed below.

Bar graphs. The bar graph is a convenient means of showing comparisons. The bar graph has two common variations. The first, and easier, is a simple comparison between two companies. Figure 1 shows a comparison between the Smith Corporation and the Walters Corporation in relation to the rate of employee turnover. Notice that the two companies are each represented by a separate vertical bar and that the companies can be compared year by year for several years.

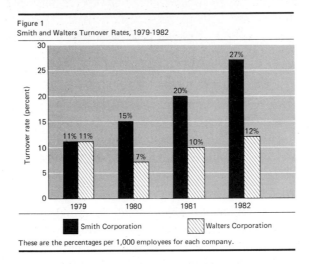

Figure 1
Smith and Walters Turnover Rates, 1979-1982

These are the percentages per 1,000 employees for each company.

This graph shows that for 1980, 1981, and 1982 Smith Corporation had a higher rate of employee turnover than did the Walters Corporation. In 1979, however, the Walters Corporation had the same rate of turnover as did the Smith Corporation.

The second type of bar graph can show positive and negative numbers. For example, Figure 2 shows the total revenue for the Walters Corporation for 1982, breaking down the revenue by each plant location.

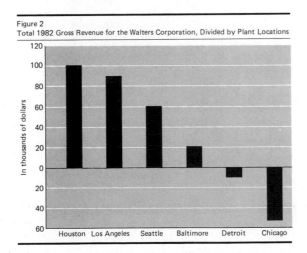

Figure 2
Total 1982 Gross Revenue for the Walters Corporation, Divided by Plant Locations

The figure shows that gross revenues were $270,000 while losses were $55,000 for a total gross revenue of $215,000. Notice that on this graph the value zero is drawn through the middle of the graph. Positive quantities are drawn above the zero line and negative quantities are below the zero line. The largest positive quantities are entered first on the left side of the graph, and the values decrease toward the right side of the graph until the lowest negative quantity is included.

Line Graphs. Line graphs can show comparisons as do bar graphs but they can also be used to show trends. Single line graphs show trends, as in Figure 3.

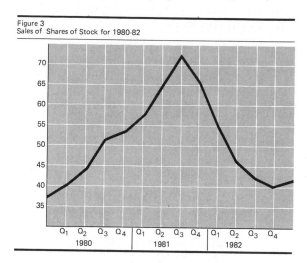

Figure 3
Sales of Shares of Stock for 1980-82

Figure 3 clearly indicates the sales of stock were slow but steadily increasing in 1980 and increased sharply in 1981. This trend completely changed in 1982 as sales of stock dropped greatly. Notice that the quantities to be plotted are given vertically on the left side of the graph. Frequently, time is plotted horizontally across the bottom of the line graph. A second type of line graph is the double line graph. This line graph shows both trends and comparisons. The graph in Figure 4 is another way of showing the same quantities displayed in Figure 1.

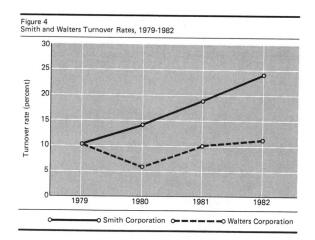

Figure 4
Smith and Walters Turnover Rates, 1979-1982

More than two lines may be used on this graph of comparison; however, using more than four lines becomes confusing for the reader.

Circle graphs. The last graph type is the circle graph. This is used only for showing comparisons. The circle (or pie) graph is divided into several parts of various sizes, all together making up a whole. Figure 5 shows the types of customers the Tips Corporation has and what percentage of the corporation's products are bought by each type of customer.

Note that this graph is very easy to read and understand. It requires little or no explanation.

When drawing this graph, always draw a perfect circle first. To determine the size of each part of the graph, multiply 360 by the percentage of each part. The result is the number of degrees the part should consist of. Remember, you must be able to add up the percentages to 100 percent.

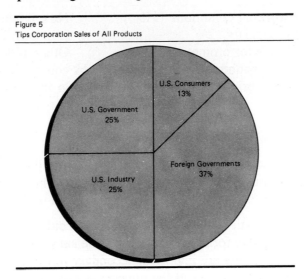

Figure 5
Tips Corporation Sales of All Products

Summary. All of the graphs are used commonly in business writing and speaking. Use them carefully, however. Use them only when they help to explain or emphasize points in your discussion. Be certain always to title each graph and label each important part of a graph. Give each graph a number as well as a title. Never use a graph without also discussing it in the article or in your oral presentation.

Practice

1. Re-draw Figure 1 using the following quantities.

Smith Corporation	10%	18%	20%	27%
Walters Corporation	5%	7%	15%	10%
	1979	1980	1981	1982

2. Draw a positive and negative bar graph for the Smith Corporation's sales for each of the following sales districts.

Detroit	$60,000	Houston	$75,000
New York	$10,000	New Orleans	$60,000
Seattle	$45,000	Tampa	$80,000

3. Create a single line graph showing the Tips Corporation's sales for 1979–82 where sales for each quarter of these years were as follows:

quarters				
1	$10,000	$60,000	$30,000	$30,000
2	$37,000	$75,000	$15,000	$20,000
3	$50,000	$50,000	$28,000	$20,000
4	$53,000	$42,000	$30,000	$35,000
years	1979	1980	1981	1982

4. Draw a double line graph comparing the information given in the first problem on the Smith Corporation and on the Walters Corporation.

5. Draw a pie graph showing the reasons for employee turnover with the following percentages:

Poor working conditions 11%	No challenge in job 29%
No job security 12%	Low pay 21%
No chance for promotion 17%	Other 10%

6. Summarize the meaning of each of these graphs you have just drawn. Write one paragraph which briefly explains the information included in each graph you have drawn.

B. Additional note taking and summarization practice

You have learned how to ask yourself questions on what you have read for the purpose of taking notes. You have also learned to find the central idea of an article and the secondary information and separate these from unnecessary information.

Reread the entire article given in this chapter. Decide what questions to ask and write the answers in note form. From among these answers, decide what the central idea is and which answers are important secondary information and which are unnecessary information. Throw out the unnecessary information. Using the central idea and the secondary information, write a summary of the article. Try to write no more than 250–300 words.

4. Action

Informal class debate

Divide the class into two teams to debate informally Adam Smith's concept of self-interest:

Team A: Adam Smith's statements regarding self-interest are actually statements about greed. The capitalist economic system is effective only because of the greedy behavior of individuals who are concerned with their own "self-interest."

Team B: Smith did not feel self-interest and selfishness were the same, and people are wrong to believe that they are. Smith meant that it is only natural that every person tries to better his own condition. Also, one person's gain is not necessarily obtained at the other person's expense.

Allow each team five to seven minutes of group preparation followed by a three-minute presentation (timed with a watch). Allow time for a rebuttal of three minutes by each team.

5. Reaction

Questions for discussion

1. The author's writing is in pure, free-enterprise, entrepreneurial terms. How theoretical is his defense of free enterprise? That is, are his statements always true when we think of the realities of doing business?

2. If it is argued that "greedy behavior" is common in a capitalistic economic system, does this mean that no greed can exist in a socialistic or communistic economic system? Does greed come from the economic system or is it a part of human nature?

3. Do you agree that "manufacturers guarantee the quality of their products by offering the value of their assets as 'hostages' to consumers who can punish opportunistic behavior"? What does the author mean by "hostage," and how may the consumer punish the manufacturer? What are the limitations on the ability of the consumer to punish the manufacturer?

4. In addition to his defense of free enterprise, what other main point is the author making? The author is with the General Motors Corporation; why would he be making these points? What restrictions or regulations have recently been imposed on the auto industry in America?

5. The author reveals a strong opinion in his article. Do you agree or disagree with his opinion? Which arguments do you think are best?

CHAPTER EIGHT: The Battle for Quality Begins

Jeremy Main

Fortune

"Quality" has a special meaning in industry. It not only indicates the excellence or superiority of a product, but often implies also the measures that must be taken in order to *control* or *assure* quality.
Reliable: dependable, which will remain in working order over the normal life of the product.
Adjustable: which can be moved or changed according to need.
Beside the point: having little to do with the subject, irrelevant.

Imperceptibly: invisibly, so slowly as to be invisible.
Clout: power, influence.
Vendors (also **venders**): those who sell (especially to manufacturers).
Periodically: now and then, sometimes, from time to time.

Assiduously: with extreme care, diligence, or persistence.
Chips: extremely small squares of semiconducting material used in micro-electronics.

Why are we suddenly so worried about the **quality** of American products? Boeing makes the best commercial aircraft in the world. International Harvester and Deere & Co. produce the most **reliable*** tractors—equipped, if farmers want, with stereos, air conditioning, orthopedic seats, and **adjustable*** steering wheels. European tourists carry off American-made permanent-press sheets because they're cheap, long-wearing, and dazzlingly patterned. Our plastics are stronger, our chemicals purer, and our machine tools built to finer tolerances than ever. This is all true enough—yet, unhappily, it is also largely **beside the point**.

America's leadership in quality has been almost **imperceptibly*** eroding for years. More and more U.S. executives have awakened to the fact that they are caught in a fateful struggle. They are turning their companies upside down to give quality specialists more **clout**. **Vendors*** are being told to supply better parts or lose the business. In hundreds of factories, small groups of workers are sitting down **periodically*** to search for ways of improving quality and productivity.

While U.S. companies have steadily improved quality, they are coming under pressure largely because the Japanese have advanced by leaps. Building **assiduously*** for 30 years on a foundation of theories developed in the U.S., the Japanese have made quality the weapon that wins the world's markets. A few bald facts show how well they have done: A new American car is almost twice as likely to have a problem as a Japanese model. An American color TV needs repair half again as often as a Japanese set. U.S.-made computer-memory **chips** were judged in one test this year to be three times as likely to fail as Japanese chips. "There's no question that the Japanese have set new world standards," says Robert E.

Cole, who has worked in Japanese factories and now directs the University of Michigan's Center for Japanese Studies. "Their best factories are better than our best factories."

Robert B. Reich, director of policy planning in the Federal Trade Commission, summarized the **consequences** of the relative decline in American quality in a speech this year [1980]: "In industry after industry, consumers in America and elsewhere are turning their backs on U.S.-manufactured products in favor of foreign competitors; 28% of our automobiles are now manufactured abroad by non-U.S. companies, 30% of our sport and athletic goods, 34% of microwave ovens, 90% of CB radios and motorcycles, almost 100% of video cassette recorders. The list goes on and gets longer year by year: radial tires, calculators, televisions, food processors, premium beer, cameras, stereo components, digital watches, pianos, bicycles, outboard motors."

Consequences: results, effects.

Among U.S. companies, it's often hard to identify the special characteristics that divide those that lead in quality from those that have fallen behind. Certainly the **pacesetters** are run by people who insist on excellence, often by an individual or family with a reputation to protect. Beyond that, though, none of the usual influences on industrial performance—**unionization***, **capital intensity*** , the number of competitors—seems to explain quality **disparities*** among companies or industries. Nor is there reason to suspect that today's makers of even the best U.S. products—farm equipment, aircraft, machine tools, large appliances—will be **immune** to future threats.

Pacesetters: those who create the standards, especially the highest standards.
Unionization: formation of associations (unions) for the purpose of supporting workers' interests.
Capital intensity: the extent to which capital must be invested per product.
Disparities: differences, gaps.
Immune: not subject or susceptible to (something), free from.

One thing that complicates thinking about quality is that the word can mean just about whatever a customer thinks it means. To the fashion-conscious, quality might mean the patch that transforms a $20 pair of jeans into a $40 pair. To a space scientist, quality represents a million parts so carefully made, tested, and assembled that they will function flawlessly for years. A **working** definition of the quality most sought today might be "fitness for use, plus reliability, delivered at a marketable* price."

Working: practical, effective.

The principles for improving quality were developed in the U.S. before and during World War II—and then **neglected** here. But Americans have been teaching the principles to the Japanese for three decades, with extraordinary results. When industrialists moved into the postwar power **vacuum** in Japan, they saw that the economy depended on **wiping out** the nation's image as the world's **purveyor** of junk. In 1950, the Japanese invited W. Edwards Deming, a Census Bureau statistician, to lecture on methods he had developed for statistical analysis of quality. Four years later, they asked Joseph M. Juran, a Western Electric quality manager, to instruct them on management's role in improving quality.

Neglected: given no or not enough care or attention.
Vacuum: a space occupied by nothing.
Wiping out: destroying, ruining.
Purveyor: seller.

Trouble in the toe department

While both men were pretty much ignored in the U.S., the Japanese honored these prophets by **devotion** to their teachings. The Deming prize for **quality control***, now in its 30th year, became so impor-

Devotion: religious attention.
Quality control (also **quality assurance**): the procedure of establishing acceptable limits of variation for products or services and of maintenance of those limits.

Beneath a quality control sign, a worker at Multiprint in New York City checks a page for errors.

Importuning: requesting repeatedly and insistently.
Imperious: overbearing, arrogant, too proud, dominating.
Fortune 500: the top 500 U.S. businesses as ranked by *Fortune* magazine.

Tally: count.

tant in Japan that the annual award is broadcast on national TV. Now, finally, American businessmen are **importuning** Deming and Juran for advice. Juran, a crusty 75-year-old, says, "I've never been busier in my life." **Imperious** at 80, Deming takes calls from **Fortune 500** companies between trips to Japan and Europe. "They want me to spend a day doing for them what I did for Japan," he snorts. "They think it is that simple. American management has no idea what quality control is and how to achieve it."

In fact, the statistical controls that Deming taught the Japanese are deceptively simple, at least in their essentials. You **tally** defects, analyze them, trace them to the source, make corrections, and then keep a record of what happens afterward. A classic case described by an associate of Deming's, Professor David Chambers of the University of Tennessee, illustrates the principle. In the 1960s, the managers of a middle-sized **hosiery** plant in Tennessee now owned by Genesco decided they had to change the ways they had grown used to in the previous 65 years. A preliminary study showed one source of defects was the "looping" department, which performed the task of closing toes. Inspectors soon found that a few of the workers produced most of the defects. An older worker responsible for 20% of the faulty loops was persuaded to take an early retirement. A dozen others did fine once they got new glasses. Another said she paid little attention to what she was doing because no one had shown concern for quality; when management did, she easily improved her work. Until recently few American companies bothered with that kind of analysis.

But a few fixes on the shop floor are rarely enough. Effective quality control—or "quality assurance" in the phrase favored by specialists today—involves the whole industrial process, beginning with product design and continuing on to the **marketplace***. In the past, American companies usually controlled quality by putting enough inspectors in the plant to **weed** defects down to an acceptable level. To people like Deming and Juran, you have already failed if you need a lot of inspectors. But the Japanese approach is **taking hold** here. "You can't inspect quality in," says Alex Mair, head of GM's technical staff. "You must build it in."

Running round the clock

Good quality demands good **tools**. A $100,000 machine that can **weld** perfect **seams** all day and night, seven days a week, without ever taking a break or complaining about the heat and noise can raise both productivity and quality. Simple automatic tools have been around for a long time, but computer-controlled **robots** that can be **reprogrammed** to do many tasks, that can "see" and "feel," that can inspect their own output, that can adjust for wear on their working surfaces, are only beginning to appear in American factories in large numbers. The five-year, $75-billion retooling of the U.S. auto industry has created a **surge*** in **demand***.

In popular imagination, the American loss of "**work ethic**" is to blame for poor quality, but specialists disagree. Under proper management, the U.S. worker is as good as anyone. In fact, some of the best German and Japanese plants are in the U.S. The Volkswagen Rabbits built in Pennsylvania and the Mercedes trucks assembled in Virginia meet German standards. Sony's San Diego plant set a company-wide record by turning out Trinitron TV sets for 200 consecutive days without producing a single operating defect.

The **turnaround** at a former Motorola factory in Franklin Park, Illinois, has become a famous example of what the U.S. worker can do. Under Motorola, the plant was literally turning out more defects than TV sets: inspectors found 140 defects for every 100 TV sets that passed along the **lines**. Matsushita Electric Industrial

Hosiery: stockings or socks.

Marketplace: anywhere that buying and selling takes place on a regular basis (often figurative).
To weed (weed out): to remove useless or undesirable (things).
Taking hold: getting started, becoming effective or operational.

Tools: implements used to do something, including equipment and machines.
Weld: join (metals) by using heat.
Seams: here, the joints between welded pieces of metal.
Robots: mechanical men, or something like them.
Reprogrammed: given new instructions (for example, to a computer).
Surge: sudden increase.
Demand: the desire to have something combined with the ability to buy it.

Work ethic: cultural tradition that a good life is one full of hard work.

Turnaround: complete change.
Lines (production lines): here, the lines of workers and equipment along which a product takes shape.

Rejects: produced items unacceptable because of defects or flaws.
Warranty: guarantee.
Eightfold: eight times; the suffix "fold" can be added to a number to indicate that many times (twofold, tenfold).

Production quotas: minimum number of manufacturing output required by management.

Cooperative: working well together.

Upgrading: raising, changing to a better quality.
Shoots for: aims for, tries for.

Blasphemy: talk that is disrespectful of anything sacred or holy.
Massive: on a large scale, of great numbers.

Exotic: not at all typical, strange, foreign.
Components: parts, pieces.
Resistor: an electrical part which reduces or lessens electrical current.
Soldered: joined with melted metal.

Co. bought the plant in 1974 to make Quasar and Panasonic TVs. The Japanese kept the same labor force and even chose Motorola's vice president of engineering, Richard A. Kraft, to be president of the new subsidiary. Kraft says the rate of **rejects** is now down to four to six per 100 sets and the number of **warranty** claims has been cut **eightfold**.

The new management made changes, large and small, on the plant floor. Matsushita repainted the walls and put the workers' names up at their places. Automation was increased, leaving less chance for human error. Most of the moving belts on the production lines were replaced with a system the workers can control. If an employee sees a problem, she (most are women) can take the time needed to solve it. She still has to meet fixed **production quotas***.

Bringing design and quality engineers, blue-collar workers, vendors, and sales and service forces into a **cooperative*** effort to improve quality is management's responsibility. Deming holds that only 15% of all quality problems are related to a particular worker or tool. The other 85% arise from faults in the company's system and will continue until that system is changed.

The contrasting attitudes of American and Japanese management offer perhaps the clearest explanation for the different quality of what they produce. Stephen Moss, an Arthur D. Little consultant who has worked with corporations in both countries, says, "The U.S. manager sets an acceptable level of quality and then sticks to it. The Japanese are constantly **upgrading** their goals." The American assumes a certain rate of failure is inevitable, adds Moss, while the Japanese **shoots for** perfection and sometimes gets close.

Imported *blasphemy*

Under pressure, American executives are rapidly changing their attitudes. Like all beginners, American managers have more enthusiasm for excellence than skills to attain it. Hundreds of thousands of Japanese have been trained in quality assurance, but only a handful of U.S. colleges offer a degree in the subject. Consultants give seminars for management, and the American Society for Quality Control puts 500 to 600 managers through its three- to five-day courses every year. But Juran thinks nothing short of "**massive** training" will do the job.

The experts like to say "quality is free." Anyone familiar with aerospace knows that isn't always so: **exotic** materials and 100% testing of **components** gobble up the taxpayer's money. Still, good quality that consumers can afford may actually reduce costs and almost always increases productivity. The earlier you detect a defect, the more you can save. Richard W. Anderson, general manager of the Computer Systems Division of Hewlett-Packard, describes the damage a faulty 2-cent **resistor** can do. If you catch the resistor before it is used and throw it away, you lose 2 cents. If you don't find it until it has been **soldered** into a computer component, it may cost $10 to repair the part. If you don't catch the component until it is in a computer user's hands, the repair will cost hundreds of dollars. Indeed, if a $5,000 computer has to be repaired in the field, the expense may exceed the manufacturing cost.

The more complicated products become, the more reliable components must be if costs are to be held down. Poor work affects expenses all along the line. In one factory Deming visited, the manager figured that 21% of the plant's capacity was tied up producing and correcting mistakes.

Looking for patient money

Because the rewards of quality assurance are hard to measure, American businessmen have been slow to appreciate them. **MBAs** looking at estimates of discounted **cash flow** don't like improvements that take a long time to pay off—even though the payoff can ultimately be enormous, as the Japanese have proved. **Stockholders** are impatient too. Japanese and German companies are financed more by **debt*** than **equity***, and the banks do not press as hard as shareholders for **inexorable** quarterly earnings gains. If U.S. corporations are to become basically quality oriented, they will need, perhaps more than anything else, patient money. They will need to rearrange the incentives that motivate managers.

It may take ten years to catch up with the Japanese, but evidence of progress is already visible. Last March, Hewlett-Packard announced the results of tests it ran on semiconductors. The failure rate of U.S. chips was five to six times that of Japanese. The news apparently shocked the U.S. semiconductor industry into action. When Hewlett-Packard ran similar tests later in the year, the U.S. manufacturers had cut their disadvantage to three to one.

Back in 1975, American color TVs failed three times as often as Japanese sets, according to one consumer survey. So last year's figure of 50% more failures represents a big improvement. After admitting frankly that the Japanese made better TV sets, Magnavox committed itself to producing a set designed for quality. The Phoenix, as it is to be called, will have 30% fewer parts than current sets. Promises a Magnavox executive: "It's going to be as good as anything the Japanese make, by design, by commitment, and by God."

MBAs: people having received Master's (degrees) of Business Administration.
Cash flow: incoming and outgoing money.
Stockholders: those who own shares in a company.
Debt: here, gaining capital for a business by borrowing money on loan.
Equity: here, gaining capital for a business by selling shares of stock in the company.
Inexorable: that cannot be resisted, absolutely necessary.

1. Business Vocabulary

A. Circle the letter next to the word or words which are most similar in meaning to the italicized term in the sentence.

1. America has almost *imperceptibly* lost its leadership in world quality.
   a. obviously, very clearly   b. not completely
   c. so slowly as to be unnoticeable

2. The number of orders for computer-controlled robots has *surged*.
   a. decreased   b. rapidly increased   c. tapered off

3. Tractors produced in America are the world's most *reliable*.
   a. cheapest   b. oldest   c. dependable

4. *Disparity* of quality is found among companies and industries.
   a. differences   b. similarities   c. dependability

5. Small groups of workers meet *periodically* to search for ways of improving quality.
   a. angrily   b. once a week   c. occasionally

6. Management's responsibility is to create a *cooperative* effort in producing goods and services.
   a. serious   b. unified, working together   c. economical

7. American tractors even have *adjustable* steering wheels.
   a. movable   b. permanent   c. soft

8. The *demand* for computer-controlled robots is rapidly increasing.
   a. price   b. number of requests for   c. outlook

9. For thirty years, the Japanese have *assiduously* made quality the weapon that wins the world's market.
   a. persistently   b. hastily   c. openly

B. Circle the letter of the choice that best completes the sentence.

1. The American auto producers are requiring better products from their *vendors*. They are putting pressure on their
   a. workers.   b. suppliers.   c. customers.

2. Japanese and German companies get most of their financing from *debt* funding. Primarily, their money comes from
   a. loans.   b. stock sales.   c. profits.

3. Workers at the Matsushita TV factory have to meet fixed *production quotas*. The workers
   a. must produce as many TVs as possible.
   b. are free to produce as many TVs as they want.
   c. must produce at least a fixed number of TVs.

4. Americans are beginning to study *quality control* (assurance). They are learning how to
   a. mass produce.
   b. produce high-quality products.
   c. control the speed of production.

5. *Unionization* cannot be blamed for the loss of quality in American products. Managers cannot say the problem lays with
    a. unification.   b. the lack of labor unions.
    c. the formation of labor unions.

6. The definition of quality is, "Fitness for use, plus reliability, delivered at a *marketable* price." The price must be
    a. competitive, salable.   b. high.
    c. established by the wholesaler.

7. Quality control begins with product design and continues on to the *marketplace*. That is, quality control continues until the product reaches
    a. the assembly line.   b. the end of its life.
    c. the seller and consumer.

8. American companies gain most of their financing from *equity* funding. Most of their money comes from
    a. loans.   b. federal grants.   c. the sale of stock.

9. Businessmen frequently look at *capital intensity* to help explain the presence or lack of quality. They study
    a. the amount of capital per employee.
    b. the amount of capital per product.
    c. the amount of capital compared to bad debts.

2. Structural Review

Past action of limited duration: Past progressive

The progressive also occurs in the past tense to express duration of a past event:

$$was/were + VB + \text{-}ing$$

Example: While the Japanese *were improving* their quality assurance programs steadily, the American companies *were achieving* short-term goals.

In recent chapters we have looked at the following progressive forms and their uses:

PRESENT	*am/are/is* + VB + *-ing*
Example:	*is looking*
FUTURE	*will be* + VB + *-ing*
Example:	*will be looking*
PRESENT PERFECT	*have/has* + *been* + VB + *-ing*
Example:	*has been looking*
PAST	*were/was* + VB + *-ing*
Example:	*was looking*

Read the selection below. Write a correct form of the verb in parentheses, using one of the four progressive tenses above.

For the last thirty years, Americans 1) _____ the principles of quality to the Japanese with extraordina[...] [...]s. The Japanese (build) _____ assiduously on a foundation of U.S[...] [...]. As a result, America's leadership in quality (erode) _____ for t[...] [...]ree decades. Before a change in management, one plant (turn out) _____ literally more defects than TV sets. Inspectors soon found that a few of the workers (produce) _____ most of the defects. One worker (pay) _____little attention to what she (do) _____. Now, however, the Japanese approach (take hold) _____ in the U.S., and U.S. executives (turn) _____ their companies upside down to give quality specialists more clout. Small groups of workers (sit) _____ down periodically to search for ways of improving quality and productivity. American businessmen (importune) _____ Deming and Juran for advice. In the future, now that pressure is increasing on American managers, many (adopt) _____ techniques that the Japanese originally learned from Americans, and more U.S. colleges (offer) _____ degrees in quality control. From now on, it is possible that American bankers (initiate) _____ more patient financing policies, and Americans (design) _____ more and more for quality.

3. Business Communications

Oral presentations

In speaking, unlike writing, the listener cannot go back to what has already been said to hear it a second time. When you speak to a group, you should make your audience understand everything you say. This means your pronunciation must be clear, your speaking must not be too fast, and your information must be well organized.

First of all, you must speak as clearly as possible. Since you speak English as a second language, it is your responsibility to make sure that what you say is clearly pronounced. Avoid too much informality and too many contractions. For example, do not say "gonna" for "going to" when speaking to a group. Also, if your pronunciation is not clear, your words may be confused by the listener.

Be sure to keep your speech fast enough that your audience remains interested, but do not speak so quickly that your listeners cannot keep up with what you are saying. For example, it is very easy to go too fast if you read directly from your notes. Reading will probably bore your audience, anyway. Always use brief notes (as discussed in Chapters Two, Three, Four, and Five) when giving an oral presentation. It is often convenient to use three-by-five-inch notecards. Using only notes, and not the full text of your presentation, will help you remember the main things you want to say while at the same time allowing you to look at your audience as you speak. By looking at your audience, you can determine whether or not they are understanding. Remember to use simple language, speak slowly, use notes to help you remember what to say, and look at your audience.

Finally, be certain that your information is well organized. You should give a very clear introduction which states (1) what your main topic is going to be and (2) what your main points will be in the course of the presentation. Then, discuss each main point in a logical, organized, step-by-step manner. Finally, state your conclusions. In stating your conclusions, you may want briefly to summarize the main points you discussed earlier.

In giving an oral presentation, you will find it helpful to remember (1) to speak clearly, (2) to use simple language, (3) to speak slowly enough that your audience understands you without boring them, (4) to look at your audience, and (5) to organize your material in a clear and logical manner.

Take notes on and summarize the article in this chapter. Then make notes on the summary (use notecards or a sheet of unlined paper). Present your summary of the article to the class in a 3–4-minute speech. After completing your speech, give your notecards to the teacher so that your notes may be evaluated for possible suggestions for improvement.

4. Action

Scenario: Management decision making

Divide the class into teams of three "managers" each. All the teams have the following problem: you manage a shirt factory which has declining output per worker, a rising number of defects per 100 units of production, and, as a result, rising per unit costs.

Among the three managers of each team, discuss the problem and make a tentative plan for correcting the problem. Consider the following in making your plans: hiring quality control specialists, tracing the defects to their source, employee retraining, showing an interest in the workers' work, redesigning the product, and buying newer and better equipment. When each group has finished its plans, they should be presented to the class as a whole. Then the class may consider the best ideas from each group and form one comprehensive plan of action to get production back to efficiency.

5. Reaction

Questions for discussion

1. The process of funding business is important. The article mentions that Japan and Germany both finance their business through bank loans, or "debt funding." American business, which has been more concerned with short-term profits than are Japanese or German businesses, finances itself rather through stock sales, or "equity funding." What is the basic difference between these two types of funding, and why do they seem to affect businesses differently? Why would equity funding make American executives concerned with short-term profits while Japanese and German executives, who use debt funding, are concerned with long-term profitability? How are businesses in your country financed and how does this affect their operation?

2. America has a history of having strong labor unions which are frequently at odds with management. Who do you think is most responsible for lacks in American quality, labor or management? What does the article seem to indicate about this problem? Support your answers.

3. The article suggests three possible definitions of quality: (1) a product with a highly respected brand name printed on it, selling at a high price, (2) a product whose parts are carefully made, tested, and assembled so that they will function flawlessly for years, and (3) a product which is fit for use, reliable, and which sells at a marketable price. How would you define quality? Why?

4. The article indicates that the U.S. has become serious about making products which will compete with Japanese and German goods. Indeed, the article points out that certain businesses have already made great improvements. What do you think will be the long-term effects on consumers of this race for quality? People all over the world buy goods produced by these three nations; how will the consumers be affected? Remember, to produce better products, better and more expensive methods of production must be used, and costs are ultimately passed along to the consumer. Also, as competition increases, how will the economies of the various nations be affected, and how will any changes affect the lives of those nations' citizens?

5. Recently some consumers have had doubts about the reliability of some American products like automobiles. At the same time, however, the U.S. auto industry has been making a major effort to recover its former share of the market by increasing the efficiency of quality control. Do you believe this effort to be successful? How will the market be divided in the future? Do American manufacturers need to make major changes? Will they make major changes? Make recommendations as to how changes might be made on the part of American industrialists to capture more of the world market.

CHAPTER NINE: Social Security Hobbles Our Capital Formation

Martin S. Feldstein

Harvard Business Review

Hobbles: for a horse, ties two legs together to prevent free movement; here, restrains, slows down.

In the past few years, the severe financial problems of the social security system have received widespread public attention. The changing **demographic*** structure of the U.S. population will make it increasingly expensive to maintain any level of **benefits***. If nothing is done to slow the growth of benefits specified in existing legislation, the social security tax rate must rise to more than 20% in the next 25 years.

Demographic: having to do with the statistics of populations, or characteristics of large groups.
Benefits: money or services that one can get because he is a citizen or because he is insured.

However important these difficulties are, they are surely less significant than the largely ignored economic consequences of social security. Most people in the business community and in government still regard social security as an expensive, but benign, transfer program that worsens our tax burden but does not materially affect the economy.

I think this view is wrong. The system exerts a substantial impact on the economy—an impact that is unintended, undesirable, and unsuspected even by the so-called experts responsible for shaping the Old Age and Survivors Insurance (OASI) program.

The most important economic effect is a reduction in the nation's rate of saving. Social security is the real root of our capital **scarcity*** problem. Although tax incentives for greater saving and investment can boost the rate of capital formation, that rate will continue at a very low level until we can reduce our dependence on social security.

Scarcity: smallness of supply compared with demand.

Let me explain why. The promise of old age benefits influences middle- and low-income workers to trim their saving. Often this reduction is achieved through explicit integration of private pensions and social security; pension benefits (and therefore previous **contributions***) fall in proportion to social security benefits. The

Contributions: here, payments.

89

*One method of reducing the growth rate of old age benefits would be
to raise the age of eligibility to age 70.*

Cut back: reduce, decrease.

Pay-as-you-go: income is used immediately
to finance the program.
Petty cash: money for small payments (not
for long-term financing).

Stockpile: store, supply stored for future use.
To offset: to compensate for, to make up for,
to balance.

reduction is also achieved directly as employees **cut back*** their
retirement saving in anticipation of government benefits.

Since the social security program is financed on a **pay-as-you-
go*** basis, the government does not accumulate the tax dollars it
receives but pays them out immediately as benefits. The government keeps only a "**petty cash**"* fund equal to a few months' worth
of payments. There are no other assets.

So when the social security system induces individuals to reduce
their saving, the program has no **stockpile*** to **offset*** the level of

private saving. And without a stockpile there can be no investment or capital formation.

The dollar significance

Let us look at how large this cut in saving is likely to be. Consider the question first from an individual's point of view. A married worker who has had the **median*** level of earnings all his life retires with social security benefits for himself and his wife equal to 65% of his **peak*** before-tax **earnings***.

Since these payments are untaxed, they replace about 80% of his maximum after-tax earnings. Moreover, the benefits are now permanently **inflation indexed** so that they maintain their real value regardless of what happens to the price level. With such a high **replacement rate**, the worker has little reason to save or to join a private pension plan.

For workers with less than median earnings the replacement rate is even higher. Because benefits are untaxed, they may in some cases exceed 100% of the after-tax income that the individuals would otherwise have earned. How strange and unfair to impose a **payroll tax*** of more than 12% on earnings during the early working years, when workers' incomes are low and family responsibilities are great, in order to finance benefits that exceed their highest income levels and that are paid after those responsibilities have been reduced!

For high-income persons the replacement rates are somewhat lower. But social security provides a significant replacement rate for all workers except the rather small number who earn much more than the current maximum taxable income of $22,900.

The replacement rate is also lower for families with second earners whose contribution to total family income is large. These groups alone still have a significant incentive to save.

For most American families social security is the most important asset. The actuarial value of the benefits to which the **breadwinners*** will be **entitled*** at age 65 exceeds the value of all other combined assets of their families. A recent study on which I **collaborated*** at the National Bureau of Economic Research concluded that the **aggregate*** value of the social security wealth of persons over age 34 now exceeds $3.5 trillion. Although no **tangible assets*** corresponding to these actuarial values exist, it is perfectly rational for individuals to regard this "wealth" as a substitute for other forms of **accumulated*** assets.

To put this $3.5 trillion figure into perspective, it is useful to note that by the most inclusive traditional measure the net worth of the private sector totals less than $6 trillion. If the current social security wealth had been saved and accumulated as real wealth instead, the nation's stock of capital would be more than 50% larger than it is today.

The volume of social security tax collections underscores the potential importance of the federal program. Since these taxes are

Median: middle; relating to the middle value in a set of numbers.
Peak: top, maximum.
Earnings: salary, pay.

Inflation indexed: designed to increase as inflation does.
Replacement rate: the ratio of pension payments to peak before-tax earnings.

Payroll tax: a tax taken directly from the salary.

Breadwinners: wage earners, those who earn salaries (usually for a family).
Entitled: having a right (to).
Collaborated: worked with (on), cooperated with (on).
Aggregate: total, collective, as a whole.
Tangible assets: of a business, its money, buildings, machinery, but not its personnel or its goodwill.
Accumulated: having been gathered or collected together.

widely regarded as a form of compulsory saving, it is revealing to compare them with private saving. In 1979 social security tax payments by employees and employers will exceed $100 billion, and all private saving will amount to about the same. Obviously, social security has a very large potential impact on the process of capital accumulation.

On the basis of evidence that several other economists and I have gathered to date, however, social security does not replace private saving on a dollar-for-dollar basis. Our studies show that each dollar of OASI "saving" reduces real private saving by more than 50 cents. This estimate is the basis for my conclusion that without the depressing effect of social security the national saving rate would be half again higher than it is today.

A way out

The long-run consequences of a reduced rate of capital formation, stemming from reduced saving, are likely to be very significant:

□ Less capital accumulation means a lower rate of growth and a lower level of income. With less capital per employee, productivity is lower and real wages grow more slowly.

□ The lack of **domestic*** saving may encourage a growing inflow of foreign investment and ownership in the United States.

□ The scarcity of capital and the inflow of foreign funds may encourage an increase in government controls over the capital markets. Unfortunately, federal credit **rationing***, guarantees, and **subsidies*** would only **exacerbate** the problem of capital scarcity by reducing the efficiency with which the existing capital stock is used.

There is a different way of looking at the adverse consequence of substituting social security pensions for real capital accumulation. In the United States, corporate investment in plant and equipment yields an average 12% return. At this rate, even a conservative estimate that the $3.5 trillion of social security wealth has cut the real capital stock by $1 trillion implies an annual loss of $120 billion of income.

Under existing legislation old age benefits are required to grow indefinitely in proportion to income. Therefore, social security will continue to replace real capital formation to at least the extent that it does today. If anything, the growth of real income and the development of formal pension integration methods will mean an even greater future impact on private saving.

A low rate of capital formation and its adverse consequences are, however, avoidable by reducing the growth rate of old age benefits in order to encourage greater reliance on individual saving and private pensions.

One method of doing this would be to raise the age of eligibility for full pension benefits to age 70 while retaining the option of retirement at any time after age 62, with payment on an actuarially reduced basis. By making the change effective some years from

Domestic: within the country, internal.

Rationing: limiting, fixing or determining quantities allowed for each person or agency.
Subsidies: money given to an industry needing help, especially by a government.
Exacerbate: make worse.

now, the government would reduce the growth of benefits without cutting benefits of the retired or those near retirement. Moreover, younger workers would pay a lower total tax during the remaining productive years.

Pressures building up

Is a shift from social security to private saving politically realistic? It is difficult to say. There are strong pressures for such a change, the most important being the serious financial problems caused by the maturity of the program and the changing demographic structure of the population.

As I mentioned earlier, the future benefits specified in the existing legislation can be financed only by raising the payroll tax to more than 20%. The experience with a much smaller tax increase indicates how much opposition is likely to a series of tax increases that nearly double the tax rate. I think that Congress will start looking for ways to avoid these increases by reducing the rate of benefit growth.

Another source of pressure toward a shift to greater reliance on private saving is the low **rate of return** that individuals earn on their OASI tax payments. This stands in sharp contrast to the experience of earlier participants in the program. Anyone who has retired or will soon retire will probably earn a very high rate of return on the taxes that he (or she) and the employer have paid.

Rate of return: the relationship between amount invested and amount of profits.

Because of the system's pay-as-you-go nature, this high rate of return reflects rapid growth—in 40 years, from 2% to more than 12%. But another sixfold* increase in the tax rate is clearly not **in the offing**!

In the offing: in the near future.

In a mature pay-as-you-go program, the average rate of return on tax payments equals the rate of growth of taxable earnings, which is between 2% and 3%. The changing demographic makeup will cause the current generation of workers to **reap** an even lower rate of return.

To reap: to harvest, to obtain a return.

Having a choice between this return and a substantially higher potential **yield** on private pensions and other forms of private saving, employees and organized labor are likely to resist the continued rapid growth of the public program and press for more private options. The possibility of protecting the benefits of retirees and older workers while permitting younger workers to reduce their lifetime contributions means that private options can be explored without hurting any age group.

Yield: return on investment, i.e. money earned by investing.

For a different reason Congress may encourage private saving at the expense of social security. Members of Congress are becoming aware of the importance of stepping up capital formation. The tax cuts in 1978, especially those on **capital gains** and corporate income, indicate that, to **bolster** capital accumulation, Congress is prepared to reject some liberal goals that have traditionally guided its behavior.

Capital gains: profit made from the investment or sales of property.
To bolster: to support, to induce.

Because of social security's financial problems, the low future rate of return on its taxes, and the new mood in Congress, the idea of slower growth of social security and a greater reliance on private saving is politically feasible. But the problems I have described are still not generally understood.

The adverse impact of social security on capital formation is poorly perceived by federal officials and the business community. The low rate of return for individuals remains hidden by the much more favorable experience of persons now in retirement. Strong institutional and ideological pressures persist to maintain the status quo by patching over the financial problems and hiding the low return through general revenue finance.

Social security is at a turning point. The next decade will require decisions affecting not only the future of the system but also the future of capital formation and economic growth in this country. Let us hope that we will not lose this opportunity for constructive reform.

1. Business Vocabulary

A. Next to each sentence write the letter of the word or words which are *closest in meaning* to the underlined word in that sentence.

A. payments
B. money received from insurance
C. lack of, shortage
D. to decrease, to lessen
E. reserve, something stored
F. compensated for, substituted for
G. middle
H. highest
I. income, pay
J. tax deducted from the salary check
K. within the nation
L. permitting of limited amounts
M. financial assistance, aid
N. six times, 600%

_____ 1. To finance future social security payments, a sixfold increase in the tax rate will be necessary.

_____ 2. A worker who has received a median salary all his life will receive about 80% of his after-tax pay in social security benefits.

_____ 3. Social security pays a significant amount of money for all workers except those whose earnings are above $22,900.

_____ 4. The median income level worker retires with social security benefits equal to 65% of his peak before-tax earnings.

_____ 5. Federal credit rationing exacerbates the problem of capital scarcity by reducing the efficiency with which the existing capital stock is used.

_____ 6. The U.S. will have difficulty in the future paying social security benefits.

_____ 7. Social security is the real root of our capital scarcity problem.

_____ 8. Foreign investments and ownership may increase as a result of lower domestic savings.

_____ 9. Social security is financed as a payroll tax.

_____10. As social security benefits go up, contributions to private pension funds go down.

_____11. Social security also influences some people to cut back their retirement savings.

_____12. The social security system has no stockpile of funds, thus there can be no investments or capital formation.

_____13. The lack of stockpile of funds means that the lower levels of private savings cannot be offset in any way.

_____14. Federal subsidies often encourage managers not to take full responsibility for capital stock.

B. Fill in the blanks with an appropriate form of one of the following words:

accumulate   petty cash
demographic   pay-as-you-go

At present the social security administration keeps only a _____ fund from which to make payments; existing social security legislation and the changing _____ structure of the U.S. population will make it impossible to _____ a larger fund, like, for example, the funds of large, private pension plans. Social security seems to be permanently on a _____ basis.

C. Fill in the blanks with an appropriate form of one of the following words as you did in the paragraph above.

to collaborate   tangible assets
to entitle   aggregate
breadwinner

"The actuarial value of the benefits to which the _____ will be _____ at age 65 exceeds the value of all other combined assets. . . . A recent study on which I _____ . . . concluded that the _____ value of the social security wealth of persons over age 34 now exceeds $3.5 trillion. . . . No _____ corresponding to these actuarial values exist. . . ."

2. Structural Review

The passive voice

The passive voice is formed by adding a PAST PARTICIPLE to a form of the verb *to be*.

Example: An error *was noticed* in the billing.

The tense of the verb is indicated by the form of the verb *to be*. In the example above, *was* is past tense, and so the entire verb is said to be in the past tense.

PRESENT TENSE Example:	Present tense of *be* + PAST PARTICIPLE Benefits *are increased* yearly.
PAST TENSE Example:	Past tense of *be* + PAST PARTICIPLE Economic consequences of social security *were ignored* for some time.
PRESENT PERFECT TENSE Example:	Present perfect form of *be* + PAST PARTICIPLE Social Security *has been regarded* by most people as a benign transfer program.
FUTURE TENSE Example:	Future tense of *be* + PAST PARTICIPLE The program *will be changed* only if there is sufficient political pressure.

Remember: the passive is formed by the correct tense of *to be* plus the *PAST PARTICIPLE*.

How does the passive voice differ in meaning from the *active voice*? In the *active voice* the subject of the sentence does the acting and the direct object of the verb receives the action. The subject is the *doer* and the direct object is the *receiver* of the action expressed by the verb.

However, in the passive voice, the subject is the receiver of the action.

ACTIVE VOICE: Congress *ignored* the economic consequences of social security.

PASSIVE VOICE: The economic consequences of social security *were ignored*.

In the passive voice, if you wish to express the *doer* of the action of the verb, you may use the preposition *by* plus the *doer*:

Example: The economic consequences of social security were ignored *by* the Congress.

However, this is not a necessary part of the sentence, and *by* may not appear at all.

A.   To gain familiarity with the forms of the passive, look at the following sentence examples and tell whether the verb is active or passive.

1. Social security is regarded by most people as a harmless program.
2. But the author claims that it has hobbled capital formation in this country.
3. The next decade will require decisions affecting the system.
4. Congress is looking for ways to avoid tax increases.
5. Benefits have been financed by raising the payroll tax.
6. Foreign investment will be encouraged by lack of domestic saving.

B.   Now choose the active or passive form of the verb in parentheses and write the proper form in the blank. In the first four sentences, the first word of the verb form has been supplied.

1. (consider)   In this article, the view that social security is benign is _____ wrong.

2. (reduced)   Social security has _____ the nation's rate of saving.

3. (reduce)   Until our dependence on social security has _____, the rate of capital formation will continue at a very low level.

4. (achieve)   This reduction is _____ directly as employees cut back their retirement saving in anticipation of government benefits.

5. (finance)   Since social security _____ on a pay-as-you-go basis, the government immediately pays out the tax dollars it receives.

6. (retain)   The government, in fact, _____ only a "petty cash" fund, without any other assets.

7. (induce)   When individuals _____ to reduce their saving, there is no stockpile to offset the lower level of private saving.

8. (replace)   In the past, the cut in saving has been large, and private saving _____ not _____ by social security on a dollar-for-dollar basis.

9. (estimate)   It _____ by conservative experts that the $3.5 trillion of social security wealth has cut the real capital stock by $1 trillion.

10. (establish)   Originally, social security _____ not _____ as a form of compulsory saving.

11. (encourage)   If nothing changes, the lack of domestic saving _____ a growing inflow of foreign investment.

12. (raise)   At the present rate the payroll tax _____ to more than 20% of its present level.

13. (create)   Pressure _____ by tax increases to change legislation.

14. (require)   During the next decade, decisions affecting the future of capital formation _____ .

15. (perceive)   Let us hope that this opportunity for constructive reform _____ clearly by the Congress and national leaders.

3. Business Communications

Conferences

Every professional spends a great amount of time in conferences (meetings). Conferences may involve only two people or many people. They may be informal conversations or highly formal group meetings. Whatever the nature of the conference, you must be well prepared.

Be certain to find out precisely what the purpose of the conference is going to be. The purpose is usually defined by the *agenda*, a list of topics in the order they are to be discussed. Are you going to clarify a problem? Plan a course of action? Make a final decision on action? Before attending always clarify exactly what the topic(s) of discussion will be.

Formulate your own objectives before the meeting. Knowing what you want out of the meeting does not, however, mean that you have to be too insistent or argumentative. You must also understand what other people want and, in some measure, compromise.

To help attain your own objectives, try to determine in advance what the others will be wanting. Prepare yourself to know not only the subject matter of the topic of discussion, but also to know the views and opinions of others in the meeting.

Finally, make written and mental notes to aid your oral participation in the meeting. Use the suggestions for oral presentations in Chapter Eight. Oral conference skills can be extremely valuable, but they are most helpful when you are familiar with the subject of the conference and the views of the other participants.

In the Action section of this chapter, you will be asked to discuss, in a conference situation, the social security system. Your teacher may require that you be in favor of or against the system. No matter which position you are asked to defend, you must be familiar with complaints against the system as mentioned in the article.

Now, review the reading, and then write a memorandum to your administrative assistant asking for all important information relating to the criticisms of the social security system. Be sure to ask your assistant detailed questions so that she/he can provide you with all the information you need. (Be certain to do this well. You will use this in the Action section).

4. Action

Conference scenario

This activity makes some use of the material you prepared in the Business Communications section. By asking your administrative assistant in a memo for detailed information on the social security system, you should have reviewed the criticisms of the system.

Divide into groups of four. Two people in each group are to be in favor of the system as it is now, and two are to be opposed to it. Those taking the position in favor of the system have the advantage of (1) knowing many of their opponents' criticisms in advance, (2) having a humanitarian point of view to support them, and (3) knowing that the system will be politically and practically difficult to change. Those against the system should make clear what it is that they propose instead (e.g., no system, a limited system, a system with a large stockpile of funds, etc.).

Each group should first discuss the pros and cons of the American social security system and any changes that might be made in it. Afterwards the class as a whole may discuss the issue on an international level, reflecting on how other nations attempt to deal with the problem of old age assistance and noting advantages and disadvantages of each system.

5. Reaction

Questions for discussion

1. What are the humanitarian considerations which make social security systems desirable? Does the existence of a social security system indicate that other institutions are not doing their job well (e.g., the family, the local communities, religious groups)? What did the aged do before social security was initiated?
2. Against what is the author's basic argument directed? The existence of social security systems? The existence of this social security system? The form of this social security system? What is it about the social security system that he thinks is disadvantageous?
3. If social security benefits are reduced in your country, what are the alternatives for those retiring?
4. How far does the responsibility of your federal government extend to social groups which lack independence (the aged, the handicapped, the sick)?
5. What are the "demographic" structural changes in the U.S. which make it especially difficult for social security to be financially sound? Is this a problem in your country?
6. Compare your country's system of care for the aged and list its advantages as well as disadvantages.

ENERGY

CHAPTER TEN: **A High-Risk Era for the Utilities**

Business Week

Skyrocketing: rising very quickly.
Slowdown: decrease in rate or speed, especially economic.

Bold: brave, courageous.
Decline: going down, worsening.
Utilities (public utility): public service industries such as suppliers of water, electricity, gas, or sometimes telephone.
Diversification: handling by a single business of widely different goods or services.
Ventures: (business) efforts in a new direction, sometimes involving risks.
Energy-efficient: which does not use much energy compared to the service obtained.

Implications: meanings, significance.
Vast: very great, very large.
Regulators: agencies (such as a board or commission) that restrict or limit (business) activity.
Crunch: time of hardship or crisis, shortage.

Tellingly: significantly, substantially.

The $82 billion electric utility industry, badly hurt by **skyrocketing** costs and interest rates and a sharp **slowdown*** in the growth of demand, is going from bad to worse. "These are the worst financial problems the industry has faced in 40 years," says James J. O'Connor, chairman of Chicago's Commonwealth Edison Co.

But as its crisis deepens, the industry is taking some uncharacteristically **bold** steps to halt its **decline***, shine up its image, and attract new capital. In increasing numbers, **utilities*** are looking for **diversification*** outside their basic business of generating and selling electric power. Their search for faster-growing, higher-profit **ventures*** is leading them into oil exploration, mining, and communications as well as into more power-related fields such as home insulation and **energy-efficient*** appliances.

The **implications*** are **vast** for both the utility industry and for a nation dependent on reliable electric power. State **regulators*** are becoming increasingly fearful that diversification will distract utility management's attention from its primary business. And although construction cutbacks are in the short-term interests of utilities and ratepayers who would otherwise have to pay the costs of building unnecessary generating capacity, the country could face a longer-term capacity **crunch** if the economy is revitalized* significantly.

Fuel supplies

Early moves toward diversification took place as much as two decades ago, when some electric utilities set up subsidiaries to develop cheap sources of fuel for internal use. Among them was Montana Power Co., and the value of its moves has shown up most **tellingly** in the last few years. Montana Power's earnings from coal and gas **shot up** 126% from 1975 to 1979 while its earnings from electric power dropped 23%. Today the company gets 44% of its total earnings from sources other than electric power, compared with 21% in 1975.

> **Shot up:** rose very quickly.

Portland-based Pacific Power & Light Co. has not only profited from its diversification into coal, beginning in the mid-1950s, but has also moved into telephone communications and is **contemplating*** getting even deeper into the business. Coal and telephones provided 51% of PP&L's total operating income in 1979—up from 16% five years before—and showed dramatically higher returns on equity than the company got from its electric power business.

> **Contemplating:** thinking about, thinking over.

Buoyed by the success of its initial ventures into telephones in the Pacific Northwest, PP&L expanded its commitment to the field considerably in 1979 with the purchase, for $200 million, of a phone company in Alaska. Now PP&L is looking hard at using this base to get into cable television. "The nice thing about the phone business," says Chairman Don C. Frisbee, "is that it has changed from an increasing-cost to a decreasing-cost business, while electric power has been going the other way."

> **Buoyed:** lifted up, raised; encouraged.

In many cases, though, reaping the benefits of such diversification requires broader management capabilities and larger capital investment than most utilities can provide. That is why many utilities are considering moves into fields more closely **aligned** with their basic business: home **weatherization**, energy consulting, and power-plant design, for example. Minneapolis-based Northern States Power Co., for instance, believes that in the future more industrial plants will use power generated on-site, and to **exploit*** this potential market, it is considering building and servicing small coal-fired boilers as a new business line.

> **Aligned:** in line, parallel, related.
> **Weatherization:** improving (a structure's) resistance to weather.
> **To exploit:** to take advantage of, profit from.

Regulators

At Duke Power Co., which has for years designed and built all its own power plants, executives are considering whether to **package** a design and construction service for sale to outside customers. Wisconsin Electric Power Co. is investigating whether it can link communications services to its existing network of wires. And along with several other utilities, Wisconsin Electric is also **looking into** using waste heat from its generating plants to warm water for fish-farming.

> **To package:** to wrap; thus, to prepare for selling.
> **Looking into:** investigating.

In its **bid** to diversify, however, the electric utility industry faces some major uncertainties. Both federal and state rules give regulators considerable **latitude** in determining what is acceptable diversification. As a result, when utilities venture into high-profit, higher-growth fields, they have no guaranteed **assurance*** that earnings from such ventures will be free from regulatory oversight.

> **Bid:** competitive effort, attempt.
> **Latitude:** range, freedom from limitations.
> **Assurance:** certainty, guaranty, insurance.

At the federal level, the Public Utility Holding Company Act of 1935 restricts the 14 utility holding companies that it governs (typi-

Why electric utilities need to diversify

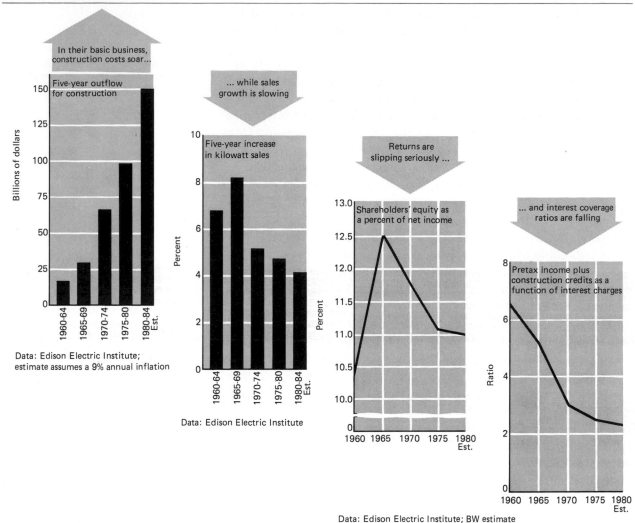

In their basic business, construction costs soar...

Five-year outflow for construction

Data: Edison Electric Institute; estimate assumes a 9% annual inflation

... while sales growth is slowing

Five-year increase in kilowatt sales

Data: Edison Electric Institute

Returns are slipping seriously ...

Shareholders' equity as a percent of net income

... and interest coverage ratios are falling

Pretax income plus construction credits as a function of interest charges

Data: Edison Electric Institute; BW estimate

Challenges: attempts to show something is wrong.
Exemptions: freedom from obligation, release.

Embarking on: beginning, starting out.
Ambitious: showing a strong desire to make progress.

cally those that own utilities in more than one state) from diversifying into businesses that are not directly related to generating and selling electric power. But in the 46 years since the act was passed, few **challenges** have been made to it. More than 100 companies have won **exemptions** from it. And in the absence of court decisions, it is unclear just how restrictive it really is.

Uncertainties

New England Electric System, for example, is subject to the act, but it is **embarking on* ambitious*** expansions into oil and gas exploration, coal transportation, and production of electronic

switching devices for electrical equipment. So far the Securities & Exchange Commission, which administers the act, has approved the oil and gas ventures and has given early nods of approval for the others on the ground that all are related to New England Electric's basic business.

There are also uncertainties at the state level. Some utility executives believe that a power company that seeks to diversify can ease troubles with state regulators by becoming part of an **intrastate* holding company**. That aim in part lies behind the recent creation of Iowa Resources Inc., a utility holding company whose centerpiece is Iowa Power & Light Co. but which also includes a coal mining operation and an industrial development arm that invests in commercial and industrial real estate. Even so, Iowa Resources' executives are not yet sure whether the holding company's earnings from nonutility businesses are sufficiently protected from state public utility regulators. "All we really know is that the new framework gives us freer activity in terms of taking risks with shareholders' money and **access*** to financing that otherwise wouldn't be available," says Mark W. Putney, Iowa Resources' executive vice-president.

While **public utility commissions** in most states do not specifically have the right to regulate nonutility earnings, they can make it difficult for a utility to hang on to such gains by **scaling back** on requested rate increases. And even now, Montana Power's executives are **fuming** over a ruling made in December by the Montana Public Service Commission that cut the utility's rate of return on the regulated side of its business by $900,000 on the **ground** that its coal-mining subsidiary had overcharged the electric utility for power-plant fuel.

A cautious approach

Despite such **hurdles**, many utility executives are still eager to get into businesses with better growth and profit **potential***. "You'll see more diversification," predicts Charles S. McNeer, chief executive officer of Wisconsin Electric, "but it won't be like jumping into the pool completely. It will be more like sticking your toes in to feel the temperature."

An as-yet-unreleased study by Booz, Allen & Hamilton Inc. also suggests this might be the course. The study found that "without assurances that the revenues of [diversification] will be **isolated from** regulatory oversight, it is doubtful that many utilities will make major commitments to these activities in the near term." It also doubts whether most utility companies have managements capable of handling business operations in unregulated markets.

Yet some that have tried diversifying have found it essential to growth. In Oregon, the very success of Pacific Power & Light's coal and telephone businesses has led to suggestions that they be

Switching devices: anything used to turn electric current on or off.

Intrastate: within one state.
Holding company: a company organized to hold the shares of subsidiary companies.
Access: availability, ease of approach or use.

Public utility commissions: the regulatory boards in each state for public utilities such as electricity, telephone, and natural gas which in many cases are public or private monopolies.
Scaling back: cutting back, decreasing somewhat.
Fuming: very angry.
Ground: basis.

Hurdles: anything in the way or that must be overcome.
Potential: possibility in the future.

Isolated from: kept away from.

Spun off: sold off, made available for purchase.

Excess: remaining, left-over, over-abundance.

Tax credits: reduction of taxes.

spun off to stockholders to attract new capital as well as protect their earnings from state regulators. For the moment, management has turned the idea aside partly because the diversifications can make good use of **excess* tax credits** generated by PP&L's electricity-producing side. But Chairman Frisbee does not rule out the idea of spinoff if diversification earnings affect the utility's basic business. "If there is evidence that the success of our other businesses is having a psychological impact on the regulators as they set our rates," he says, "it would not be in the shareholders' interest to maintain the company as a whole."

Battered: damaged, beaten.

Because of the electric utility industry's **battered** financial condition, there are plenty of utilities that would like to diversify but cannot, either for lack of new capital or because they have committed all available capital elsewhere. One prime example is Detroit Edison Co. It faces payments of $3 billion in construction costs from now to 1985. Says John W. Johnson Jr., financial vice-president at Detroit Edison: "With our present [power-plant construction] commitments, we just can't afford the kind of big investment it would take to swing a favorable return for our stockholders."

Spreading the risks

Capacity: ability to deal with demands.

Comes on stream: begins operation (industrial jargon).

Kw: kilowatts; 1,000 watts, the international unit of power.

Dallas-based Texas Utilities Co. faces another common problem in the industry—too much generating **capacity***. It began a major building program in 1974, and when its newest nuclear plant **comes on stream** in 1984 it will be able to generate about 1 million **Kw** more than the estimate of a comfortable reserve margin at the time.

To head off: to stop before it is too late.

Escalation: increase (sometimes large).

Many other utilities were able to move sooner to **head off** or delay construction programs begun before the **escalation*** of fuel costs that led to the decline in the growth in demand for electric power in the U.S. The National Electric Reliability Council, which keeps track of generating capacity, reports that 18.5% of the total new generating capacity due to come on stream from 1976 through 1985 will be delayed until 1989 and that a further 18.7% will be delayed even longer or canceled outright.

Joint: mutual, cooperative.

Those utilities that are continuing to build projects on schedule are finding new ways to spread the risk. To share costs and reduce exposure to further slowing in the growth of demand for power, many are participating in **joint** projects or selling off shares in their completed projects. Before 1976 only 6.3% of the nation's generating capacity was in jointly owned facilities; today that has grown to 9.9%.

Project financing

Burden: something that is carried, load; responsibility.

Imposes on: forces on.

Savviest: cleverest, most able or knowledgeable.

To ease further the **burden** that the high cost of new construction **imposes on*** balance sheets, many utilities—and their investment bankers—are seeking new methods of financing. Among the **savviest** in both its public and private placements has been Cleveland

Electric Illuminating Co., which in 1977 **pioneered** utility financing placements in the Middle East and last April began selling $60 million in small-denomination bonds to the public through Merrill Lynch, Pierce, Fenner & Smith Inc.

Such financing deals, however, do not win **wholehearted endorsement** from industry executives. Some view them as no more than cosmetic **coverups** of the utility industry's ill health. Says James M. Henderson, chairman of Central Louisiana Electric Co.: "You can do these things maybe once, but ultimately you must get back to the fundamentals. These don't solve the electric industry's long-term problems."

Conservation

Up to now, the public's response to higher electric power costs has been to cut back on use. Short-term, this simply **intensifies*** the financial pressure on the utilities by lowering revenues they receive to cover their **fixed costs***. But in the long run utilities may become eager to encourage conservation because it could cut their need to spend for new capacity.

In most states, regulatory commissions are also **pushing** electricity conservation. This is especially so in California, where utilities have been ordered to hold energy growth to 1.5% annually and to finance low-cost loans to their customers for insulation and energy-saving equipment. Often, though, state commissions that preach conservation also encourage utility expansion by matching rates to a utility's spending for new plant. This angers some utility executives. Bertram Schwartz, senior vice-president at New York's Consolidated Edison Co., complains bitterly that the New York State Public Service Commission "**feverishly** promotes conservation but doesn't seem to reward utilities for doing it."

The most aggressive **proponent*** of conservation among utilities is probably Pacific Gas & Electric Co., the San Francisco–based utility that will pump $164 million over the next 10 years into dozens of programs that will contribute to cutting its peak demand by 25% by the year 2000. Savings from such a reduction can be striking. Con Edison, for example, estimates that its conservation efforts have saved it from buying some 30 million **bbl.** of imported oil since the Arab oil embargo of 1974. And Wisconsin Electric, which five years ago began an effort to halve its annual increase in demand, estimates that it has eliminated* $1.5 billion in future construction costs.

"A matter of survival"

If that trend continues, however, it will turn the electric utility business upside down. The appetite of the consumer will no longer determine the growth of power capacity; instead, growth will be determined by a utility's ability to finance new capacity. "We will

---

Pioneered: was the first (to do something).

Wholehearted: sincere and energetic.
Endorsement: approval, support.
Coverups: acts of disguising, concealing, or hiding.

Intensifies: makes stronger.
Fixed costs: amounts paid out which do not change or cannot be changed.

Pushing: encouraging, supporting.
Feverishly: very excitedly but not very reasonably, as in a fever.

Proponent: an advocate, a supporter, one who proposes or suggests.
bbl.: barrels.

Plague: trouble, bother greatly.
Dip: go down suddenly.

Curtailed: cut off from electric services.
Blackout: sudden, temporary loss of electricity to an area.
Tradeoffs: corresponding advantages or disadvantages likely to be experienced in the future.

control what the [economy's] growth rate will be by our ability to produce," admits Richard E. Disbrow, president of American Electric Power, the nation's largest investor-owned utility holding company.

Serious problems could develop from this. Electric power shortages could stymie efforts to revitalize the country's basic industries. And by the end of the decade, continuing shortages could **plague** many areas of the U.S. as reserve margins **dip** from today's national average of 33% to a dangerous 18%, and even lower in such areas as the Pacific Northwest and the Southwest.

Henderson of Central Louisiana Electric, which will slash its reserve margins from 30% today to 15% by the end of 1982, admits as much. "Right now," he says, "the customer doesn't know he has been **curtailed***. But when the first **blackout** comes, he'll rise up in arms. Then we'll have to do our best to explain the situation we were facing." Says Gary L. Neale, president of Planmetrics Inc., a consultant to 62 electric utilities: "In 10 years, if there are shortages, the utilities will simply have to say that they did the best job they could given the resources they had. In many cases it's survival now *vs.* **tradeoffs** later."

1. Business Vocabulary

For each sentence given below, words are provided in parentheses. Put the proper form of the correct word in the blanks.

> Example: (utilities, imply, slowdown, escalate) One of the
> <u>implications</u> of <u>escalating</u> crude oil costs is a <u>slowdown</u>
> in the growth of demand made upon the <u>utilities</u>.

1. (ambition, energy-efficient, embark) Also, appliance producers are _____ upon _____ plans to produce _____ appliances.
2. (curtail, fixed costs, potential) While _____ remain high for producers of electricity, consumers are _____ their demands for electricity which in turn lowers the utility companies' _____ for profit.
3. (capacity, revitalize) Many utility companies are attempting to _____ their poor financial structures by cutting _____ .
4. (eliminate, proponent, excess) Wisconsin Electric, one of the _____ of energy conservation, has been able to avoid having _____ capacity and has actually _____ $1.5 billion in future construction costs.
5. (diverse, decline) The industry is taking bold steps to halt its _____ by looking for _____ outside its basic business.
6. (contemplate, exploit) After _____ further _____ of the communications industry, Oregon's PP&L expanded its commitment by buying, for $200 million, a phone company in Alaska.
7. (venture, regulate, assure) One problem is that the utilities have no guaranteed _____ that earnings from these _____ will be approved by _____ .
8. (access, intrastate) One of the benefits of becoming part of an _____ holding company is that it gives utilities _____ to financing that would be otherwise unavailable.
9. (intensify, impose) While energy conservation helps cut back on crude oil imports, it _____ _____ financial pressure upon the utilities by lowering revenues.

2. Structural Review

The passive voice (cont.)

Some major forms and uses of the passive voice were discussed and practiced in the exercises of Chapter Nine. Carefully review these in order to increase your skill in the following more difficult exercise.

Complete the sentences with an appropriate form of the verb in parentheses. All the answers in the exercise will be in the passive voice in one of the following tenses: present, future, past, present perfect, and past perfect. No progressive tenses are necessary. As in the exercise in Chapter Nine, the auxiliary is provided only in the first four questions. After that, you must provide both the auxiliary and the past participle.

(to look for)   1. Today it is commonplace when diversification is _____ outside the utilities' basic interests.

(to take)   2. Sometimes they are _____ by their leaders into home insulation and energy-efficient appliances.

(to expand)   3. By 1979, PP&L's commitment had _____ considerably.

(to provide)   4. At that time, a much larger percentage of PP&L's total income was _____ by coal and telephones.

(to show)   5. In fact, much higher returns on equity _____ by these interests than by the electric power business.

(to change)   6. The phone business _____ from an increasing-cost to a decreasing-cost business.

(to investigate)   7. Soon, the possibility of linking communications services to existing networks of power lines _____.

(to generate)   8. In the future more on-site power _____ at industrial plants.

(to acquire)   9. But too much generating capacity _____ by some companies in recent times.

(to win)   10. In 46 years, over 100 exemptions from the Utility Holding Act _____.

(to suggest)   11. Nevertheless, it _____ that diversification will be slow among utilities.

3. Business Communications

The letter of application

When one applies for a position with an American company, the letter of application cannot and should not contain *all* the information a prospective employer wants to know about you. The resumé (to be discussed in Chapter Fifteen) will accompany your letter of application, and this is where most of the details about you will appear. The letter of application should serve as a supplement to the resumé.

You may begin your letter of application by stating exactly what work you are seeking. Be very specific about this. If you know of a job opening within the company, refer specifically to that position. Also, if some person from that company told you of the job opening, you may want to begin the first paragraph by mentioning this person by name. At any rate, you should begin your letter by mentioning the job you are seeking and perhaps by mentioning your source of information about the job.

The second paragraph is important because this is where you tell more about yourself than the resumé can tell. In this paragraph you should try to distinguish your application from all others. Here, you may elaborate on some job experience or training which does not stand out on the resumé but which may particularly qualify you for the job. Be careful not to make this paragraph too long. Like all good business communications, the letter of application must be concise and to the point.

To help you write the second paragraph, find out all you can about the company and the job opening before writing the letter. If you can make specific reference to the company's needs and how you can fulfill them, your chances of getting a job interview will be much better.

Close the letter with a request for an interview. Be careful to clearly state your desire for an interview and your willingness to accommodate their schedule in arranging the interview.

The overall tone of the letter should be pleasant and honest. You do not want to attempt to over-impress the employer with your talent or knowledge. If you do have unusual knowledge or ability, your resumé and references will make this clear; you do not need to push this in the letter. A pleasant and sincere attitude will reap the best results.

Review the sample letter of application given below. After studying its various sections and tone, write your own. In writing this letter, assume you are writing to some specific company for a specific position. With the information given in this chapter, you may want to write to one of the utility companies mentioned in the chapter, explaining how you may be of service to them (some of the utilities needed managers while others needed investment bankers).

January 23, 19—

2987 E. Peach St.
Dallas, TX 74639

Ms. Joan B. Willis
Personnel Department
Diamond Oil Company
New York, NY 10003

Dear Ms. Willis:

I have spoken with your Dallas representative, Mr. James Schultz, and he informed me that your company is in need of someone having an FCC Communication Technician license. I should like to submit my application for the position requiring this license.

As my resumé indicates, while working for the Magnolia Oil Company, I have used my FCC licensed technical skills for eight years. In fact, I was among the first Magnolia technicians to receive this training. Not only did I use my training in performing my work duties, I also served as an in-house trainer for those technicians planning to apply for FCC licensing. In the course of these eight years with

Magnolia Oil, I have gained experience with most of the electronic testing and maintenance equipment used in the oil industry.

Please refer to the enclosed data sheet for details on both my education and work experience. There you will also find the names of persons willing and able to comment on my ability and character.

Because of the extreme distance between Dallas and New York, I will be glad to interview with your Dallas representative or with you by telephone. I can arrange either at your company's convenience.

Respectfully,

Mark T. Riley

Enclosure: Resumé

4. Action

Panel discussion

The public utility commission in the state where you live is holding hearings across the state for the purpose of educating the public about the problems the utility companies are facing. The commission also wants the public to know how these problems may affect the supply of electrical energy in the future. The hearings are held in the form of panel discussions. The panels will include a representative from the state regulatory commission, a representative from one of the utility companies, a consumer, a consultant for the utility industry, and a moderator.

Divide the class into small groups to discuss the problems of the utility companies. Each student should take the role of one of the panel members mentioned above.

1. *The representative from the state regulatory commission* will understand the financial problems the utilities are having while at the same time he will worry about the possibility that diversification will distract utility management's attention from its primary business. He will have to answer questions from both the utility company and from the consumers.
2. *The representative from the utility company* will have to explain that fixed costs remain high and fuel costs escalate while revenues decline due to the users' conservation efforts. He wants to defend the idea of diversification by explaining that it is the only way the utilities can solve their financial problems.
3. *The consumer* will be primarily concerned with keeping rates low and will be worried about the cutback in construction. The planned cutbacks will mean that less energy will be available in the future, and when less is available, it will probably be more expensive.
4. *The consultant* will be interested in supporting the utility industry's interests in diversification. He will want to convince the regulator and the consumer that diversification is the best solution. He will support himself by using facts and figures.
5. *The moderator* will be the person to keep the discussion lively. He will try to

confront the utility representative and the regulator as well as the consumer and consultant with various questions or issues which will be difficult for them to answer.

Each member of the panel should review the article to prepare his own brief statement for the audience and be prepared to enter into a general discussion once the individual presentations have been made. Additional panel members may be added if the class sees the need. The moderator will introduce the panel topic and the panel members and will begin the discussion.

5. Reaction

Questions for discussion

1. View the problem from the consumers' point of view. Can we trust the utilities when they say they are having financial problems? True, they do have fixed costs, but the rates they charge us are not fixed and continue to climb. The utilities have no competitors; we have no choice who we buy our electricity from, so the companies do not have to worry about losing customers even when their rates increase. Can we really believe they need to diversify, or is diversification only another way for the utilities to make more money?

2. How ethical is it for electricity producers to be getting into the business of mining coal? Many of the electrical power generating plants are fueled by coal. This means that some of the utility companies will not only produce electricity, but they will produce the coal which produces the electricity. The potential problem is that these companies could set their own rates for coal prices and could artificially increase the price they charge for electricity as a result of higher prices for coal. If this were the case, the consumer would lose, and the utility companies would benefit greatly. Would the regulatory agencies prevent this from happening? Recall the example of the Montana Power Company.

3. Do you foresee the possibility of large corporate users of electricity generating their own electric power by means of owning coal-powered generators? If this were to happen on a wide scale, would this mean that only individual (home owners) customers would eventually be the ones buying electricity from the utility companies? If this were so, would it necessarily be bad for the consumer?

4. Consider the utility industry in your own country. Do any of the problems in the article apply to your country now or possibly in the future? How would the problem be dealt with there? If the problem could not occur, why is this so?

5. The article discusses the move that some utility companies are making toward cutting back on construction and using the money saved to invest in other businesses. Such investment helps the companies' financial position. However, future energy growth is limited by this strategy. Until now, the consumers of electricity have always determined the amount of electricity produced. In the future, the growth of electric consumption will be determined by a utility's ability to finance new capacity. The utility companies will control what the economy's growth rate will be. Is this a desirable situation? How much power will the utilities have over the growth of the economy?

CHAPTER ELEVEN: Energy Conservation: Spawning a Billion-Dollar Business

Business Week

Spawning: giving birth to.

Conserving: saving, keeping from loss.
Consumption: use, using up.

Phase: point, period or step in development.
Stage: point, period, or step in development.

Growth industry: a line of business that is rapidly expanding throughout the market.

Recessionary: due to slowing in business activity.
Shutdown: closing, stoppage of operation.

Conserving* energy was never regarded all that seriously as a primary method for cutting the nation's appetite for imported fuel. But a growing mass of data indicates that energy conservation will be a more important factor in holding down the nation's energy **consumption*** than many observers had expected.

While conservation obviously cannot solve the nation's long-term energy problems on its own, such efforts are slowing energy consumption far more than even the most optimistic forecasts and have graduated from the turning-down-the-thermostat **phase** to a second-**stage** effort. This is being fueled by an accelerating capital investment in new energy-efficient equipment and booming sales in conventional conservation products such as insulation.

Indeed, this conservation drive is now creating a **growth industry*** in products aimed at conserving energy. Spending for energy efficiency last year amounted to $8.7 billion—twice the amount spent in 1979 and more than the combined spending of the preceding five years. Most analysts expect the total investment to top $10 billion this year and soar to $30 billion by 1985.

"Conservation has taken hold much faster and produced larger savings than anyone could anticipate," says Lillian W. Deitch, vice-president of Futures Group, a Glastonbury (Conn.) consulting company. The latest figures tend to back her statement. In January, the Energy Dept. reported that energy efficiency in the 10 most energy-intensive industries—which include steel, aluminum, and chemicals—improved 15.4% since 1972. Overall production by these industries increased an average of 20% while their energy consumption dipped 2.2%, which translates into a savings of nearly $1 billion annually based on the present price of crude oil.

Although these figures may also reflect the **recessionary*** shut-

down of older and less efficient plants in such industries as steel, analysts are convinced that conservation efforts have accounted for a significant part of the energy saving. They argue that the sudden surge in conservation efforts began in mid-1979, when the real price of energy jumped after several years of increases that failed to keep up with the rate of inflation. "It is a perception thing," declares Harvard University economist Dale M. Jorgenson. "People realize that energy will never be cheap again."

That decision by homeowners and companies alike to begin investing more money to get more out of their energy dollars is causing many energy analysts to **revise*** their forecasts. In late March, for example, the Energy Dept. decided that energy consumption would grow at a rate of 1% a year through 1990. Less than two years ago, it **pegged** the rate at 3%. Similarly, most of the major oil companies—including Shell, Exxon, Atlantic-Richfield, and Conoco—have lowered their **estimates*** of **projected** energy demand. Exxon Co. USA now forecasts that energy consumption at the turn of the century will be fully 34% less than what its economists had predicted in 1972. And a study to be released shortly by the Mellon Institute's Energy Productivity Center foresees virtually no growth in energy consumption through 1990 and a rise of only about 1% annually in the next decade. Further conservation could affect even these bright predictions. "Even the most optimistic projections we're making today may be **understating** conservation's real potential," says Roger W. Sant, author of the Mellon study.

To revise: to reconsider, to correct.
Pegged: marked, determined.
Estimates: approximate calculations.
Projected: estimated, forecast, predicted.
Understating: saying that something is less than it is.

Room for growth

Even more surprising is the fact that most of the current projections allow for a modest rate of economic growth. Exxon expects that the **GNP** will move along at a 2.6% growth rate, compared with the 4% **clip** of the 1960s. The Mellon group anticipates a similar rate accompanied by no energy growth at all. Indeed, there are indications that GNP and energy consumption may be breaking out of the **lockstep** in which they have **marched** in the past. The ratio of GNP to energy use is changing at an accelerating rate.

GNP: gross national product: a country's total annual value of goods produced and services provided.
Clip: rate, speed.
Marched in lockstep: walked together in disciplined, military style.

Tougher challenges

The easy steps toward conserving energy have already been taken by the industry. But industry is taking the harder steps by investing in new equipment and technology. At the same time, home owners are investing more in such items as storm windows, insulation, and caulking. The Energy Dept. **maintains*** that the energy consumed by the average home could be **slashed** 60%.

Already, a conservation industry to supply the products is taking shape. At least 178 companies, for example, are marketing some type of computer-controlled energy management system for commercial buildings. These systems typically slice 25% or more from energy bills by **maintaining** temperatures and lighting conditions

Maintains: states as true, asserts.
Slashed: greatly reduced, lessened, or cut.

Maintaining: keeping, holding, retaining.

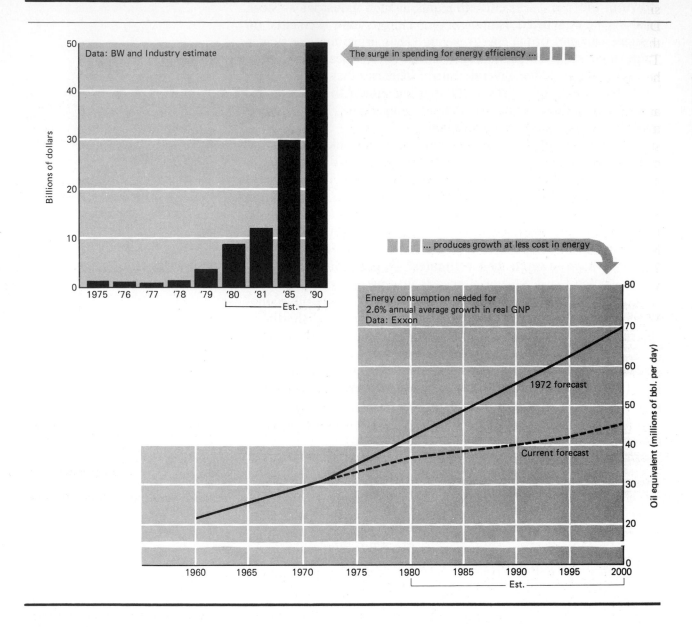

Data: BW and Industry estimate

Billions of dollars

1975 '76 '77 '78 '79 '80 '81 '85 '90
Est.

The surge in spending for energy efficiency ...

... produces growth at less cost in energy

Energy consumption needed for
2.6% annual average growth in real GNP
Data: Exxon

1972 forecast

Current forecast

Oil equivalent (millions of bbl. per day)

1960 1965 1970 1975 1980 1985 1990 1995 2000
Est.

Sensors: devices which detect a change or receive a signal.

for various work areas at different times of the day. By connecting **sensors** located throughout the building to a computer, the systems automatically adjust heating and cooling to take into account all heat generated by machines, lights, and people. They also control lighting by sensing the amount of sunlight in an area and the number of people working there.

The market for building management systems is expected to grow from $300 million annually today to $1.8 billion by 1990. Honeywell Inc., the largest supplier, has sold more than 7,000 systems since the 1973 oil embargo. A Cambridge (Mass.) company, Count Digital Inc., recently began marketing a similar system for the home that can be used with home steam or hot water heating systems. The system costs $2,000 and is said to be capable of reducing home heating bills in the Northeast as much as 40%.

At the same time, nearly 1,000 "energy stores" have popped up around the country in the last couple of years, ready to provide **audits*** for residences and install energy saving products from insulation to high-efficiency heating systems. Last year home owners claimed tax credits on an estimated $4 billion and estimates are that such **expenditures*** could amount to $30 billion a year by 1990. "We're seeing a need and we're filling it," says Jackson S. Gouraud, a former Deputy Energy Under Secretary who is president of Energy Clinic Inc., headquartered in Westport, Conn. By next year he boasts that he will have expanded his five-store operation into 280 stores nationwide, with sales of $250 million. "Energy conservation is no longer a **corner store** operation," he says.

More than a dozen companies, including Du Pont, Ebasco, and Westinghouse, are offering similar services to industry. "There is no shortage of customers," says Wallace W. Carpenter, vice-president of energy conservation at Ebasco Services Inc., which established a conservation consulting section in 1979. Since then, it has done more than 100 audits for hospitals, chemical companies, and other factories.

The number of new products and processes being introduced that are aimed at improving energy efficiency is growing rapidly. Westinghouse Electric Corp., for example, which already markets industrial **heat pumps** to **recover** waste heat, is bringing out a new line of energy-efficient motors and analyzers and metering equipment for measuring and controlling **combustion** efficiency. Other companies, such as A. O. Smith Corp., a Milwaukee manufacturer of bicycle and automobile frames, are attempting to diversify into energy conservation products. A. O. Smith has begun to market a heat **recuperator** that can recover as much as 20% of the heat that now goes up industrial smokestacks.

Sales of such products are already **on the upswing**. Moreover, companies are lining up to buy products that would have sounded like science fiction only a few years ago. Novitas Inc., a privately held Santa Monica (Calif.) company, makes an **ultrasonic** sensing device that turns off lights when no one is in the room. Although the unit sells for $110, the four-year-old company suddenly is **inundated** with orders. "Before, people were interested in the concept but didn't buy any," says James D. Himonas, president. "Now, they are ordering them in quantities of 500 or more." Among Novitas customers are Hughes Aircraft Co. and Memorex Corp., which has racked up energy savings of 45% with the device.

"Energy conservation is becoming a big market" for the producers of pumps, compressors, computers, and other components of

Audits: examinations, evaluations.
Expenditures: expenses, what is paid out.
Corner store: formerly, there were small stores, or shops, on many corners in American towns. Thus, the idea of the common small-business man.

Heat pumps: devices for transferring heat from a substance at a lower temperature to one at a higher temperature, as for a building.
To recover: to get back, to recuperate.
Combustion: burning, the processes associated with oxidation.
Recuperator: a device which recovers something.

On the upswing: on the increase, increasing.
Ultrasonic: of a frequency too high for the human ear.
Inundated: flooded.

Predicts: foretells, says in advance of the event, estimates for the future.
Retrofitting: equipping after the fact (after plants are in place).

Turbine: engine which is turned by water, steam, or air.

Spurred: given life, motion, energy.
Mw: megawatts.

To forestall: to stop or prevent before it is too late.

Blitz: sudden, strong attack.

Boggled: astounded or amazed.

Stepping up: increasing, increasing the rate of.

energy-efficient manufacturing equipment, says Steve C. Carhart, who heads Carhart Associates, a Washington (D.C.) consulting group that advises companies on energy-saving equipment. Carhart **predicts*** that over the next five years industry could spend as much as $60 billion **retrofitting** its plants with energy-efficient components. Most of that recycles waste, burns trash as fuel, recaptures waste heat, or utilizes process steam.

A double play in steam

One older technology getting a lot more attention these days from industry is cogeneration, which uses steam twice, for heating and running a **turbine** to generate electricity. Cogeneration was widely used by industry 50 years ago but was largely replaced by cheap power from utilities.

The market for cogeneration is being **spurred*** by a 1978 law that requires local utilities to buy excess power from industrial generators. As a result, industry experts predict that there will be 1,000 cogenerators in use in the U.S. by 1990, triple the 350 in use today. Mellon Institute pegs the 1990 market for cogeneration at $18 billion. General Electric Co., which is the leading manufacturer of turbines used in cogeneration, expects that as much as 50,000 **Mw** of power will be cogenerated in the U.S. by the end of the century.

GE, in fact, is planning to install as many as six cogenerators at its own plants at a cost of $50 to $100 million each. Northeast Utilities recently found that companies in its service area could cogenerate as much as 200 Mw, and it plans to encourage conversion to **forestall*** having to add capacity to its own system. "It is starting to make good economic sense for the utilities," says former Representative Wilbur Mills (D-Ark.). He represents Arkansas Power & Light Co., one of a group of utilities seeking tax credits so they can do their own cogeneration.

The potential market for cogeneration and other technologies to improve the energy efficiency of U.S. industry has not escaped the notice of foreign companies that, because of costlier energy in their countries, have long experience in improving the energy efficiency of their industry. Nearly a dozen foreign manufacturers, including Sweden's FVV Group, have set up U.S. subsidiaries in the last two years. In Britain, the London Chamber of Commerce recently launched a drive to boost U.S. sales of 1,700 British companies either consulting or manufacturing energy conservation equipment. The companies plan a unified marketing **blitz** in the U.S.

"The U.S. market could be unlimited," declares Jacques C. Vaast, vice-president of marketing for France's Montenary International Corp., a Paris company that recently opened a New York office after two years of offering conservation consulting services in Montreal. "We were sizing up the U.S. market from Canada," says Vaast, "and the size of it **boggled** our minds."

At the same time, however, U.S. industry is **stepping up*** efforts to develop new technology. Since saving just one barrel of oil a day would cut a company's fuel costs by $15,000 annually, there is plenty of incentive to carry out more energy-related research and development. The Energy Dept. estimates that energy-intensive industries are spending an average of 55% of their **R&D** dollars on improving energy efficiency—an amount that exceeded $5 billion in 1980. Aluminum Co. of America, for one, has **allocated*** two-thirds of its $87 million R&D budget in 1981 for energy conservation and energy-related projects. This includes development work on a smelting process that the company believes will ultimately reduce energy consumption by 25%.

R&D: research and development.
Allocated: distributed, assigned.

Similar efforts are already **paying off*** for some companies. Union Carbide has developed a process for producing polyethylene that requires only one-quarter the energy of existing plants. That new technology has all but rendered existing polyethylene capacity **obsolete**, and the company's competitors are negotiating for licenses to use the process. Exxon Corp. recently became the first licensee and others will follow shortly, according to Union Carbide officials.

Paying off: giving profits, being a profitable business.
Obsolete: out of date, old fashioned, not up to date.

The Tennessee Valley Authority's National Fertilizer Development Center in Muscle Shoals, Ala., has developed a process that cuts energy consumption by 60% in **turning out*** granulated nitrogen fertilizer. Some 27 plants have already been retrofitted at a cost of $20,000 each, saving $150,000 worth of natural gas annually.

Turning out: producing.

The quest for capital

Energy conservation is becoming so important to energy-intensive manufacturers, in fact, that those without ready access to capital could be in trouble. "The potential for further energy reductions is directly **proportional** to the amount of money available," says Richard L. Apensen, energy management director at 3M Co. and chairman of the energy conservation committee of the National Association of Manufacturers. "And energy-intensive companies have a real **cash flow*** problem," he says.

Proportional: having to do with the relationship of one quantity or size to another.
Cash flow: incoming and outgoing money.

The average **rate of return*** on sales for most energy-intensive industries is only about 3.9%, leaving little capital available for new equipment and developing new processes. "There are some companies that I fear might just not make it as a result of their inability to raise enough capital to do the needed conservation work," says Douglas G. Harvey, who heads the Office of Industrial Conservation in the Energy Dept. He worries about U.S. companies losing out to foreign competition.

Rate of return: the relationship between amount invested and amount of profits.

The Japanese steel industry, Harvey notes, produces steel with as little as half the amount of energy per ton that their U.S. **counterparts** use, largely because their plants are based on more recent—and more efficient—technology. "There is no way, with that kind of disadvantage, that an American company can compete," he says. "It becomes kind of a **Catch-22**, because there are very few places where [the U.S. companies] can secure the kind of capital

Counterparts: persons or things closely corresponding to or acting like another.
Catch-22: a problematic situation with no solution.

needed for an all-out assault." At the same time, some experts are concerned that the huge amounts of capital required to improve the efficiency of U.S. plants could offset the benefit of energy savings to the economy.

Unquestionably, those companies with capital are committing their resources to energy conservation. "Any [expenditure] to save energy that is wasted can be justified," says Stanley B. Reynolds, Jr., senior adviser in Exxon Chemical America's feedstock and fuels department in Houston. Adds energy consultant Carpenter of Ebasco: "The same companies that wouldn't talk to us a year ago are on the phone now all the time."

1. Business Vocabulary

A.   Rewrite each sentence below in a way that clearly shows the meaning of the word in italics. Do not use any form of the italicized word.

>   Example: Americans are successfully reducing their energy *consumption*.
>
>   Americans are successfully reducing the amount of energy they use.

1. Energy analysts are having to *revise* their forecasts of energy consumption.
2. The Energy Department *maintains* that the energy consumed by the average home could be slashed by 60%.
3. *Expenditures* by home owners could amount to $30 billion a year by 1990.
4. The article points out that federal laws can *spur* a market for certain products.
5. The major oil companies have had to lower their *estimates* of projected energy demand.
6. Rises in the cost of oil have created a billion-dollar business in *conserving* energy.
7. The Tennessee Valley Authority's Fertilizer Development Center has developed a process which *turns out* a fertilizer while using 60% less energy.
8. Industry experts are *predicting* that there will be 1,000 cogenerators in use in the U.S. by 1990.
9. American industry is *stepping up* efforts to develop new technology.

B.   Choose the most appropriate term from the following list to complete the sentences. Use each term one time.

estimates	recessionary	rate of return
pay off	cash flow	growth industry
allocating	forestall	audits

1. Many plants in such industries as steel had to close down when the economy entered a _____ period.
2. Some of the new energy-related businesses provide _____ of homes and install energy-saving products.
3. In its search for new technology, Aluminum Co. of America is _____ a larger part of its R&D budget for energy conservation.
4. Most energy-intensive industries have only a 3.9% average _____ on sales.
5. Energy-intensive industries frequently have problems with _____.
6. Because of increased energy conservation, businesses have had to lower their _____ of energy demand.
7. The utility companies are encouraging energy conservation in an effort to _____ building additional capacity.
8. The concern for energy conservation has created a new and dynamic _____.
9. Many companies, like Union Carbide, find that their efforts to create new technology _____ financially.

2. Structural Review

Indirect discourse: Reporting what someone stated

In order to report what someone has stated, you may use quotation marks (DIRECT DISCOURSE) or a clause introduced by *that* (INDIRECT DISCOURSE).

DIRECT DISCOURSE Example:	*Business Week* stated, "Conservation efforts are slowing energy consumption."
INDIRECT DISCOURSE Example:	*Business Week* stated that conservation efforts *were slowing* energy consumption.

Commonly in reporting someone's statement the main verb is in the past tense: He stated . . . , She reported . . . , Mrs. Arnold replied. . . . Notice that in the *that*-clause, present tense verbs are changed into the past tense so that they will be in the same tense as the main verb, as in the above indirect discourse example. This is called "back-shifting" the verb. Look at the following examples:

DIRECT DISCOURSE Example:	The author said, "This conservation drive is creating a growth industry."
INDIRECT DISCOURSE Example:	The author said that this conservation drive *was creating* a growth industry.

Note that verbs in other tenses are also back-shifted to a tense further into the past:

DIRECT DISCOURSE Example:	Lillian W. Deitch said, "Conservation has taken hold much faster than anyone could anticipate."
INDIRECT DISCOURSE Example:	Lillian W. Deitch said that conservation *had taken hold* much faster than anyone could anticipate.
DIRECT DISCOURSE Example:	Dale M. Jorgenson declared, "People realize that energy will never be cheap again."
INDIRECT DISCOURSE Example:	Dale M. Jorgenson declared that people realized that energy *would* never *be* cheap again.

The word *will* is back-shifted to *would*, and *can* is back-shifted to *could*.

If the statement is universally true in the past as well as in the future, then the verb in the *that*-clause may not be back-shifted (but it is usually permissible to do so).

DIRECT DISCOURSE Example:	John said, "Conservation is never a bad idea."
INDIRECT DISCOURSE Example:	John said that conservation *is* never a bad idea. *Or* John said that conservation *was* never a bad idea.

Change all the following direct discourse statements into indirect discourse.

1. At one point the Mellon study reported, "Even the most optimistic projections understate conservation's real potential."
2. The energy management director at 3M Co. said, "Energy-intensive companies have a real cash flow problem."
3. *Business Week* reported, "The market for building energy management systems is expected to grow to $1.8 billion by 1990."
4. The interviewee declared, "Already, a conservation industry to supply the necessary products is taking shape."
5. The author wrote, "Many producers will benefit as conservation becomes widespread."
6. He continued, "Nearly 1,000 'energy stores' have popped up around the country in the last couple of years."
7. Northeast Utilities stated, "Companies in the surrounding service area can co-generate as much as 200 Mw."
8. Exxon stated, "Energy consumption at the turn of the century will be fully 34% less than 1972 predictions."
9. One official from the Energy Department said, "There is no way that an American steel company can compete with more efficient Japanese technology."

3. Business Communications

Case study

The *case method* of the study of business is commonly used in graduate and undergraduate business training. It requires study of one specific example of a business problem which typifies a wider business problem of concern to the students. After considering the *case* (example) presented, the student should be able to apply knowledge gained to his own business needs.

The aim of such case study is to propose the best possible solution and to defend that solution as strongly as possible. Typically, the solution is written in a special report form, which includes consideration of the following:

1. *Background*—a short summary of the most important information found in the case. This acts as an introduction to the next section.
2. *Statement of the Problem*—a concise statement of the major problem.
3. *Discussion of the Problem*—a lengthy discussion of all information related to the main problem; discuss here, also, the point of view from which you are going to be studying the problem (i.e., are you taking the position of a manager, consultant, or employee).
4. *Alternative Solutions*—a list of all possible solutions to the problem.
5. *Analysis of the Alternatives*—an analysis of each of the alternative solutions stated above. Note the advantages and disadvantages of each.

6. *Selection of the Best Alternative*—an explanation of which alternative you have selected and why it was chosen.

7. *Implementation*—an explanation of how the solution is to be put into effect.

Divide the class into small groups (two or three students) and study the job interview case given below. Think about the questions given at the end and, as a group, write a formal solution to the case.

Case study

Mr. Mark Powers is a graduating senior at the University of Michigan. His major has been English. On the advice of the college placement office, Mark called a publishing company named Overstreet to set up an interview for an entry-level proofreading position which had been advertised in the placement center's newsletter, *Job Line*. The main requirement for the position was the ability to find errors in material to be published.

For the last two years, Mark has worked as a part-time proofreader and writer for the university press. Both his work experience and his educational experience were listed in detail in the resumé which he had prepared to take along with him to the interview.

Mark arrived early for his interview with John Hart, chief editor for Overstreet. He was dressed in a dark suit and shined shoes. Mr. Hart was dressed casually.

Mr. Hart began the interview by asking Mark to describe his school work and his work experience. Mark did most of the talking, being interrupted by Mr. Hart only when he got too far from the topic of the job. Whenever Mr. Hart interrupted, he asked about Mark's experience with word processors, copy-editing, and page composition.

Mark knew little about these things because other people at his job at the university press had performed these duties. He said he believed that these kinds of duties were "technical and required no real creative talent." Mark suggested to Mr. Hart that he read a recent issue of a popular magazine which discussed the creative talent needed to be a writer, even a writer of good letters and reports.

The last half hour of the interview was taken up with Mark's discussion of his work and his favorite poets. Both he and Mr. Hart shared an interest in poetry, and they discussed some of the modern American poets. The discussion was very friendly, and the interview, an hour long, ended on a very friendly note.

Two weeks later, Mark received a letter in the mail thanking him for the interview and explaining that he did not get the job.

1. Why do you think Mark did not get the job?
2. List things that Mark could have done differently at the interview.
3. Should a formal letter of application and a resumé have been sent to Mr. Hart before the interview?

4. Action

Job interview

Data Count is a growing company which develops, manufactures, sells, and maintains environmental control systems used in office buildings and hospitals. The systems sold by Data Count monitor room temperatures and lighting in all areas of a building. The use of such a system can save hundreds of dollars in energy use annually.

Data Count is searching for a representative to make initial contact with building managers and hospitals. Once a system is installed in a building, the representative is to stay in touch with the building manager, making sure the system operates correctly. If any malfunctions occur, it is the representative's job to make sure that the service section of Data Count corrects the problem. Such a person would need to have a pleasant disposition and would need to have some familiarity with the system and its maintenance.

Three people are interviewing candidates for the job. One person is the vice-president of operations. He is in charge of sales, engineering, and maintenance. At the interview he does not have much to say directly to the candidates; he mainly listens. The second person is the manager of sales. He wants to be sure they select someone with whom he can work. He also wants to be sure the person has the type of personality needed for making initial contact with building managers.

The last of the interviewers is the manager of engineering and maintenance. He is interested in the candidate's technical knowledge.

The three interviewers just described will interview each other member of the class. All but these three, then, will play the role of job candidates. If the class is large, two groups of interviewers and candidates may be selected to work at the same time.

Allow the interviewers five minutes to plan questions they may wish to ask and information they may wish to give the applicants. These five minutes can be used by the applicants, also, to prepare for the interview.

Allow five minutes for each interview.

When all the interviews are completed, the interviewers should select the best candidate for the job and report to the class as a whole why they selected this applicant.

Make the interviewing process as realistic as possible.

5. Reaction

Questions for discussion

1. The article says that Americans never regarded energy conservation seriously as a method of cutting the "nation's appetite for imported fuel." However, the article does not discuss why Americans felt this way. Why do you think Americans have historically disregarded energy conservation? What motivates people in your country to conserve energy?

2. The shortage and expense of oil have helped to create a new and growing industry in the design and production of energy conservation. Therefore, the world has gained new and better technology as a result of this shortage. However, the world has also gained political tension and conflict as a result of the shortage of oil. As we can see, the oil shortage has affected all nations in a variety of ways. Discuss the many and various effects, both economic and political, of oil shortage.

3. The article discusses the problem of energy-intensive industries needing capital for new equipment and technology. These industries, though, characteristically have cash flow difficulties. As an example, the steel industry in the U.S. cannot afford the new technology it needs to compete with the Japanese steel industry, because the new equipment it needs is too costly. What can be done to help these industries which are energy-intensive and cannot afford new equipment? Many of these industries, like the steel industry, are important to the overall economy of a nation. Consider what actions could be taken by banks and by the government.

MANAGEMENT

CHAPTER TWELVE: "Invisible" Resource: Women for Boards

Felice N. Schwartz   *Harvard Business Review*

*Despite the increased appearance of women on corporate **boards** in recent years, only 1.8% of the directors of the top 1,300 boards are women. Almost without exception, these women have been highly **"visible"** for their achievements in government, education, and nonprofit circles. But there are hundreds of other high achievers who are not so visible. The problem for chairmen and **nominating committees** is twofold: (1) identifying and selecting the best of this "unknown" but talented **pool*** of candidates and (2) defining and communicating their **expectations*** from women.*

Boards: (board of directors) group of persons controlling a business.
Visible: here, outstanding, prominent, well-known.
Nominating committees: groups who suggest possible representatives or members (in this case, board members).
Pool: common fund, supply, or service, provided by or shared among many.
Expectations: wishes or confidences of something to be done, produced, or received.

Women have only recently entered the boardroom. The popular perception is that large numbers have been appointed to corporate boards and that they are now a significant presence on the boards of most major corporations in the United States. But that perception does not yet reflect reality.

It is true that the number of women directors in the United States has increased dramatically, from 147 in 1976 to 300 in 1979, but the ratio of female to male directors remains remarkably small: there are only 300 women directors on only 365 of the Fortune "1,300" boards, whereas there are about 16,000 men on these boards.

This new phenomenon of the woman director is interesting; pressure to recruit women directors, unlike that to employ women in the general work force, does not **derive** from legislation. The 935 companies among the top 1,300 that do not have women on their boards are not subject to **penalty***.

Derive: to have as a starting point, source, or origin.
Penalty: punishment for failure to obey rules or keep an agreement.

But the pressure to recruit women directors is nevertheless real and recognized. It comes primarily from **stockholders***, from employees (in particular from women employees, especially those at high levels), and from consumers. This pressure reflects a growing

Stockholders: those who own shares in a company.

Corporate responsibility: the idea of duties that a company is legally or morally obliged to carry out, such that it may be blamed if it does not.
Accountability: responsibility; the expectation of having to give an explanation.
Expertise: specialized knowledge or ability.
Chairmen: (chairman of the board): the highest ranking board members.

Preferences: which is better liked or rather chosen.

Specifications: instructions for the design and materials for something to be made or done.
Directorships: the positions held by board members.
Chief executive officer (CEO): officer holding top position in any administrative hierarchy, with duties of advising and directing organizational policies and of acting as liaison officer between the administrative and legislative bodies.

Perspective: point of view; the ability to look at things from different points of view.

widespread concern with equal employment opportunity, a tendency to broaden definitions of **corporate responsibility***, and a demand for greater **accountability*** on the part of both director and company.

On the other hand, the incentives to appoint women to boards have not yet been clearly perceived. The contribution expected from women directors and the characteristics, perspectives, and **expertise*** required to make that contribution have not been adequately analyzed. The fascinating thing is that the contribution expected from women directors has not yet been defined either by corporate **chairmen*** and their nominating committees or by the women candidates for those positions.

I will explore four separate aspects of the problem:

1. The **preferences*** of the chairmen.
2. Making a contract with the woman director.
3. The challenge for women directors in the 1980s.
4. Selecting women candidates.

The chairmen's preferences

Specifications for **directorships*** have traditionally been loosely drawn. One thing that has been fixed, however, is that the **chief executive officer** has always been the most desirable candidate. Every CEO I have talked with would like at least a half-dozen chief executives on his board. When the chairmen of the large corporations began to be interested in recruiting women for their boards, they sought women in their own image—chief executive officers. Such women, however, are rare today.

The second preference of chairmen who became interested in recruiting women was often a woman who had the equivalent—or nearly the equivalent—of CEO experience. The boards of the top ten companies in the *Fortune* "1,300" do not include a single male from business who is not a chief executive, a former CEO, or the equivalent.

The chairmen's third preference then became women of high achievement outside the business world and preferably—but not necessarily—from an area that would yield insight, **perspective***, and experience obviously relevant to the concerns of the corporation. Such women tend to be highly "visible" and accessible; 120 of the 300 women currently serving on the top 1,300 boards are from government, education, and the nonprofit sector.

The chairmen's first three choices—women chief executives, women with CEO-related experience, and women of high achievement outside business—virtually exhausted the supply of *visible* women.

The corporate problem is that the pool of qualified women candidates as currently perceived, is inadequate. Thus, two things must happen: the visible pool of candidates must be enlarged, and expectations of them must be clarified.

*The number of women directors in the U.S. has increased, but the ratio
of female to male directors remains remarkably small.*

Making a contract

The area of board responsibility has been vastly expanded. A greater
range of experience and an infinitely broader perspective are needed
today than in the past. The **sine qua non*** for directorship can no
longer be chief executive experience or the equivalent. It must now
be the highest level of intelligence and motivation. There is no
shortage of either among women. However, the chairman's expectations of the new director must be realistic, clearly analyzed and
defined, and well communicated to her. She, in turn, must agree to
accept the responsibility to fulfill those expectations.

In effect, a contract, based on the board's need for a particular
perspective or expertise and a woman's ability to perform, must be
made between the chairman and the new director. Realistic **ground
rules** would thereby be established so that the woman could make
the needed contribution to the work of the board and derive both

Sine qua non: an essential element, condition that cannot be done without.

Ground rules: guidelines established so that
things wll run smoothly to be understood by
everyone concerned.

Spectrum: range, scope, variety.
Role models: examples to be imitated.

professional satisfaction and the respect of her peers from the contribution she makes.

There is a wide **spectrum** of significant yet different contributions that women directors have been able to make, from their specialized corporate experience as well as from their valuable experience in the public sector. Another valuable contribution that many women directors can make is to enhance the morale and the productivity of women in their companies, not only by their presence on the board as **role models** but by communicating actively with them and thus understanding and addressing the special needs and problems women face. Moreover, on the horizon is an enormous role that women can perform on boards by helping to analyze and seek solutions to the problems of the two-career family. The forward-looking chairman has this in mind in recruiting new directors for his board.

One positive aspect of women's presence in the boardroom is that their desire to learn and their position as representatives of a new phenomenon have allowed them to ask questions more freely than men, whose history of participation has led to the assumption that they are more knowledgeable about matters discussed and issues raised than they necessarily are.

Transition: gradual or formal change.

For both men and women, the move from a functional position to the position of director entails a shift from a primary concern with management to a primary concern with policy. Many outside male directors also face a necessary **transition** in perspective.

On the way up the corporate ladder, when the needed expertise and perspective are both in place, the signals are clear. No conflict about the nature of the function one is paid to perform occurs. But when the transition is made from staff to board, the woman needs guidance and encouragement from the chairman.

Concessions: something admitted, granted, or allowed especially after discussion or a difference of opinion.
Applaud: express approval of.

I would not argue that less should be expected from women or that they should seek special **concessions*** as women. I would urge, however, that if the contribution of some women is what has been traditionally viewed as a "female" contribution (e.g., in the areas of corporate social responsibility), the chairman should **applaud** her for it—and encourage her to applaud herself for that contribution.

If, however, the contribution of some women is what has been traditionally viewed as a male contribution, they should be equally applauded. In short, the challenge of the chairman is to ignore gender and encourage all the strengths women have to emerge and express themselves in the boardroom.

The challenge for women

Permeable: that can be passed through.

The wall surrounding the corporate community, if it can be claimed to exist at all, is today a highly **permeable** one. Just as a degree of regulation by government and the voices demanding greater accountability are growing, so the corporation recognizes that it must be increasingly concerned with the environment in which it functions and with the human as well as the consumer needs of the people.

It is true that conditions are changing in many ways, but it should be remembered that most directors, of both sexes, are over 50 years old. They grew up in a highly **polarized** society. Women learned that the traditional role of women was to maintain the home and to work, often as volunteers, in efforts to improve the community. The majority of men were **socialized** quite differently so that they would perform the function of ensuring the financial well-being of their families.

Polarized: concentrated around two opposite or contrasting positions (here, contrasting ideas about the roles of men and women).
Socialized: adapted to the needs or requirements of society, especially as one grows up.

This difference is reflected in the career development of most of even the outstandingly successful women of the generation now in their fifties. It is reflected in the careers of women now on corporate boards: 25% are in education and 22% are in government, law, and the nonprofit sector.

Women are thus uniquely positioned to perform this function, *not because they are women*, but rather because they are joining boards now at a particular time. "They are," as Fletcher Byrom, chairman of Koppers, says, "a group whose time has come."

By serving as a bridge between the corporation and the community and having an understanding of the one within the context of the other, women can bring new perspectives and responses to the role of the corporation and the conduct of business.

The Catalyst[1] program

In its nonprofit role, Catalyst is expanding its concern with women directors through a program designed to help women bring new insights to corporate boards.

The Catalyst Women Directors' Program, for which Revlon, Inc. has provided funding, will help business be more responsive to the changing needs of society by:

● Raising awareness about emerging society issues that may affect the business community.

● Serving as a channel of communication between corporate leaders and those who are leaders in thought and action on these issues.

● Providing a **forum** for sharing knowledge about these issues.

● Acting as a **sounding board** for government and business.

Forum: occasion or place for exchange of views or knowledge.
Sounding board (or sound board): a means for causing an opinion or plan to be widely heard.
Symposia (plural of symposium): conferences for discussion of a subject.

The program will, in this its second year, invite corporate, government, academic, financial, and international leaders to participate in a series of **symposia**, each focusing on a topic of crucial significance to the corporate world. Some examples include long-term inflation, increased government regulation, the aging population, and the energy shortage and their effects on business.

A company's ability to be responsive to social change is no longer solely a matter of corporate conscience. The effectiveness of a cor-

[1]Catalyst, of which Ms. Schwartz is founder and president, is a national nonprofit organization that promotes the productive utilization of women in corporations and the professions.

Constituencies: groups having a special interest and power (direct or indirect) over someone.

poration in coping with external factors and society's needs affects how it is perceived by its key **constituencies*** (i.e., by its customers, employees, and investors) and how well it can implement its corporate strategies over time. Social change is no longer a matter merely for charitable attention but has become a factor that can influence a company's growth and even survival.

The Women Directors' Program, in acting as a channel of communication between corporate leaders and leaders in other fields, serves corporate society both by helping it to anticipate emerging social issues and by enhancing the special contribution that women directors individually and as a group can make to the boards on which they serve.

Selecting women candidates

Network: here, an informal organization of like-minded persons (for example, women) who help each other advance in status or position; "old boy network" refers to the informal organization of men who have long been in the same kind of business, think alike, and do favors for each other, especially getting better pay and position for each other.

Identifying and choosing women for corporate directorships is difficult. Although there are approximately 3,500 women whose achievement and/or level of employment might qualify them for consideration as directors, the vast majority are unknown to most corporate leaders. In addition, the **network** through which they might be reached—the "new women's" equivalent to the "old boy" network—has not yet been widely established.

Dossiers: collections of various papers for a specific purpose, especially for showing and describing the qualifications of a candidate for a job.
Cross-indexed: referred from one part of a file to another. In this case, you could look up female candidates by geographic location or field of work.

The Catalyst Corporate Board Resource (CBR), which is chaired by Coy G. Eklund, president and chief executive officer of Equitable Life Assurance, whose own board includes four women, represents an attempt to organize just such a network along rational, objective lines. Catalyst has researched and identified a comprehensive national collection of accomplished women who are potential candidates for corporate boards. CBR currently contains the **dossiers*** of 837 of the most outstanding women in the country, dossiers **cross-indexed** by geography and field.

Accomplished: skilled, well trained.

In a sense, CBR was launched before its time, insofar as the supply of well-known, **accomplished** women was sufficient to meet the early, limited demand. However, in the years ahead, it is likely that the movement to recruit women directors will accelerate.

Currently 365 corporations, including every one of the top ten, have added women directors. Of the corporations, 2 have four, 5 have three, and 50 (including 1 of the top 10) have two.

Expedite: speed up the progress of; help along; assist; facilitate.
Assimilation: absorption, integration, becoming a part of another group.

It has become difficult to think of a board without women. Two factors will further **expedite*** the process of **assimilation**:

1. The disappearance of the novelty of having a woman on the board.

2. The recognition of the contribution women can make, with the clarification and realization of the incentive to recruit women that I mentioned earlier.

In the former connection, one of the most delightful comments I have heard is from Alice F. Emerson, who said:

"I didn't realize how strange I looked to the other directors until a second woman was added and sat across from me at the table."

1. Business Vocabulary

A. Circle the letter of the choice which best completes the sentence.

1. Unlike discrimination laws, there is no *penalty* for not having women on a company's board. Companies without women on the board do not receive
   a. money.   b. governmental assistance.   c. punishment.

2. Corporations must think about their key *constituencies*. They must consider the desires of
   a. the directors.   b. leaders in government.
   c. various groups connected with the company.

3. Corporate *expectations* from women directors must be clarified. They must define
   a. how to select a woman.   b. the results wanted from women.
   c. the woman's qualifications.

4. The author does not want special *concessions* made for women directors. She does not want chairmen to
   a. give women special privileges.   b. disregard women directors.
   c. treat women equally.

5. Women offer a special *expertise* to corporate boards. Women can provide a board
   a. a new point of view.   b. efficiency.
   c. unique knowledge.

6. The author notes two points which will *expedite* the process of women entering the boardroom. She lists two factors which will help
   a. keep women out of the board room.
   b. speed up the process of getting women into the boardroom.
   c. make entering the boardroom difficult for women.

7. The *sine qua non* for directorship can no longer be chief executive experience. Having been a CEO can no longer be
   a. the primary condition.   b. required.   c. expected.

B. Complete the sentences with an appropriate form of the word in parentheses.

1. (prefer)   The author lists several _____ held by chairmen when selecting a board member.

2. (stockholder)   _____ are part of the constituencies of the corporation.

3. (account)   More and more, corporations are being held _____ for their actions.

4. (pool)   The Catalyst program is an effort at _____ the names of women qualified for membership on corporate boards.

5. (chairman)   _____ must learn to disregard the gender of the individual board members.

6. (dossier)   The Catalyst program compiles _____ on the various women capable of being corporate board members.

7. (director)   The job of the director, that is, the _____,
                     needs clearer specification.

8. (corporation,   Women can help define _____ _____
   responsible)   in times of social change.

9. (perspective)   Women are able to enhace the ability of a board to
                     be accountable for the full range of corporate
                     activities and responsibilities because of their
                     unique _____ .

2. Structural Review

Hypothetical situations

Sometimes it is necessary to express a hypothetical situation or to imagine a "condition contrary to fact." This may be done by joining two clauses, one introduced by the word *if* and followed by a verb in the past tense, and the other containing *would* plus an infinitive:

(*If* . . . + PAST TENSE VB)

(. . . *would* + INFINITIVE . . .)

The clauses may come in either order. Look at the following example:

Example: *If* the stockholders *exerted* more pressure on their
             companies today, more women *would become* board
             members tomorrow.

or,   More women *would become* board members if
             stockholders *exerted* more pressure on their companies.

Remember that *if* + PAST TENSE VERB expresses a *present* condition. (Past conditions will be discussed in the next chapter.)

The verb *to be* is a special case. In an *if*-clause, use *were* when you would expect to use *was*.

Example: If I *were* you, I would hire her.

The normal past tense form of *to be* would, of course, be *was*. To express an imagined condition, English uses *were* instead of *was* in formal English. In informal English (and in many business contexts), *was* is frequent and perfectly acceptable.

A.   Complete the following sentences using the following list of possibilities:

   a. were clearer to them.
   b. were more widely recognized.
   c. were accepted by all involved.
   d. had women board members.
   e. had grown up in a different kind of society.
   f. were a man.

1. Women would be in greater demand as board members if women's contributions to business . . .

2. Companies generally would tend to recruit more women board members if the incentives to do so . . .

3. Present board members would have less difficulty in dealing with women board members if they . . .

4. Dr. Newcomer would be a director today if she . . .

5. Everyone's expectations for women board members would be met only if a set of ground rules . . .

6. The women employees would have better role models if the company . . .

B.   Likewise, complete the sentences below using the following possibilities:

    a. would have to recruit more women directors.
    b. would never know of their existence.
    c. would need guidance and encouragement like any other person undergoing such a transition.
    d. would be appointed immediately.
    e. would have greater chances of becoming board members.
    f. would recruit more women directors.
    g. would be expedited.

1. If Ms. Sobran were a CEO, she . . .

2. If the new women's "network" were more widely established, these women . . .

3. Even if there were more women qualified to become directors, most companies . . .

4. If women on the board of directors were not considered unusual, the process of assimilation . . .

5. If companies clearly foresaw enhanced morale among women employees, they . . .

6. If Ms. Taylor were changed from staff member to board member, she . . .

7. If companies with no women board members were subject to penalties, they . . .

3. Business Communications

Telex and TWX messages

Business engaged in frequent external communication must look for the most practical means of communicating. In addition to mail and telephone, Telex and TWX (teletypewriter exchange) sending/receiving systems are widely used.

Telex and TWX communications offer several advantages. They are rapid: the message is sent immediately, like a telephone call. Also, they provide both the sender and the receiver a printed record of each message. These two advantages combine the most desirable elements of both telephone call and letter.

There are also cost advantages. Generally speaking, Telex and TWX messages are inexpensive. Charges are made by the minute, but the resulting cost is about one cent per word. The TWX is even cheaper. Both machines print at the end of the message exactly how much time was used in sending the message. Thus, the user is immediately provided with a statement of costs for each message. This, of course, is useful in accounting for expenses and budgeting. As a result, Telex and

TWX communication systems are highly desirable as a means of communicating across long distances, since they provide written records of all correspondence and costs and communicate quickly and economically.

In order to write good Telex or TWX messages, some basic principles should be observed. Since long messages are more expensive, you will want to conserve words and to be as concise as possible. However, if your message is so short as to be unclear, it is wasted expense. Similarly with abbreviations—a careful use of abbreviations is helpful in reducing message costs, but overuse of them will prevent your reader from understanding, and will in the end result in costs of additional communications and lost time.

Ordinarily there is a form to be used for writing your message. Below is an example form. Look it over. The blank after "Charge to" is used if the cost of the message is to be charged to a customer's account—that is, if a customer is paying for it. The other blanks are self-explanatory.

TELETYPE SENDING BLANK

Date _____   Time _____

Charge to: _____   TWX# _____

Destination: _____

To: _____   From:_____

Subject: _____

_____

_____

_____

_____

_____

_____

End/Closing _____

The following are some sample common abbreviations:

A/C = account; NO = number; REF = in reference to;
QUTYS = quantities; GAL = gallons; CC = carbon copy.

Study the examples given and try writing your own Telex/TWX message on the suggested problems. Remember to be brief but clear: omit words where you can, but only if the omission will not prevent the reader from understanding you. Complete sentences are rare in Telex messages.

Example 1

FROM: HANCOCK SHIP AGENCIES, KOBE, JAPAN, 3/5/8–

TO: BLACKSEA SHIPPING – BLACKSEA, U.S.S.R.

CC: HANCOCK SHIP AGENCIES – NEW YORK

100 GAL ETHYLENE GLYCOL LOADED WITH TEXACO AT HOUSTON. WILL ADVISE OTHER QUTYS LOADED LATER WHEN KNOWN. SUNOIL CONFIRM CAN LOAD ONLY 400 GAL ETHER ACETATE. REGARDS

FIELDER (sender's name)

HANCOCK

ELAPSED TIME 00:01:07

Example 2

FROM: MGB INDUSTRIES – CARACAS, VENEZUELA

TO: GENERAL DATA, HOUSTON, TEXAS 9/4/8–

REMITTED TELEGRAPHICALLY US DOLLARS 15,629 CENTS 32 TO YOUR A/C NO 083949 WITH BANK OF SOUTHWEST HOUSTON BEING REMITTANCE FOR SECTION C OF CONTRACT 8472 ON SUPPLY OF TERMINAL DISPLAY ELEMENTS. PLEASE INFORM SOONEST OF SUPPLY DATE TO CARACAS. REGARDS

MALDONADO (sender's name)

MGB

ELAPSED TIME 00:02:05

Problem 1: Your company is Thermostrong, in New York. Your client, Osio Industries, in London, sends you a message confirming that your account in a local bank has been credited in the amount of $3,487 U.S. for producing and delivering instruments used in the measurement of high-level temperatures. Osio wants the products as soon as possible. You both agreed to this amount in contract number 9327 dated May 6, 198–. Answer Osio's message.

Problem 2: Your company, Sachs Incorporated, has its main office in Los Angeles, California, with a branch in Singapore. Your company imports cloth and jewelry. Your name is Booth, and you are trying to learn why your branch in Singapore is late in delivering two shipments of cloth. Your customers in the U.S.

need the cloth and are asking you about it. You send the message on February 20. A carbon copy is to go to Sachs office in New York.

Problem 3: You are the person in the Sachs Incorporated office in Singapore. Your name is Leong. You are answering Booth's inquiry, telling him about both shipments. The first was sent by sea on a ship named the "Viking" on February 8, 198–, and should arrive in Los Angeles by March 15. The second shipment will be sent by air within the next four to six days on Singapore Airlines. You will try to have it in Los Angeles by February 27. You are answering on February 20. You want a carbon copy sent to the New York office.

4. Action

Informal class debate

Divide the class into two teams to debate the qualifications for directorships:

Team A: Women who are candidates for directorships must be former CEOs or should have the equivalent experience of a CEO. Candidates must be highly visible. Women's potential contributions must adhere to traditional roles for directors.

Team B: The *sine qua non* for directorship can no longer be chief executive experience or the equivalent. Intelligence and motivation are more important. The contributions expected from women directors must be analyzed and defined.

Allow each team five to seven minutes of group preparation followed by a three-minute presentation (timed by a watch). Allow time for a rebuttal of three minutes by each team.

5. Reaction

Questions for Discussion

1. The author of the article suggests that chairmen should make a special effort to encourage women board members to make whatever contribution they can, whether it be "feminine" or "traditional." How realistic is it to expect chairmen actually to make this special effort? If you were to speak with a chairman on this subject, what arguments could you use to persuade him that such a special effort is worthwhile?

2. The author refers to the idea of the corporation's social responsibility and suggests that this is an area where women board members can make significant contributions because they have been socialized to have such concerns. She is speaking of the situation in the United States. What are the possibilities for

women in top management positions in other countries? Are there specific qualities that women have in other nations which would qualify them to make special contributions to their companies?

3. In addition to providing the board with an awareness of social responsibility, the woman director also provides a role model and moral support for women of her company. Some nominating committees look for women specifically with the ability to make these two kinds of contributions. Is there a danger that women who are very capable in all aspects of corporate affairs will be limited by the other board members to "feminine" contributions?

4. Outside the U.S., do you know of similar efforts to encourage women to become involved in top positions in business?

CHAPTER THIRTEEN: **Small Business Discovers Its Strength**

Arthur Levitt, Jr.

Business Week

Lobby: a group of private persons who try to affect law making.

Entrepreneur: individual who goes out on his own to start or run a business, small businessman.
A good head for: to have a good ability to do something.
In the black: making a profit; traditionally, black ink is used for credits and red ink for debits.
Collective voice: unified opinion.

Overstatement: saying too much.
Representatives: persons authorized or empowered to act for another or others.
Conference: meeting for consultation or discussion.
On the verge of: near, about to.
Breakthrough: a sudden, impressive improvement.

Delegates: people appointed and sent for a purpose (usually to a meeting).
Got the word: heard a piece of news.

For the first time in American history, small-business men and women throughout the land are about to become the most powerful political **lobby** in the country.

The backbone of the American enterprise system has always been the ambitious **entrepreneur*** who wants to be in business for himself or herself and with drive, imagination, innovation, salesmanship—and **a good head for** staying **in the black**—manages to make his or her way in our competitive system. But it is the chief executive officer of the big corporation who has had the loudest voice in regard to national economic policy. Now all that may change. We will be hearing much more from the **collective voice** of the local florist, stationer, travel agent, restaurateur, who together constitute more than 14 million small business entrepreneurs in the U.S.

A sympathetic ear

Is this an **overstatement**?

I do not think so. Anyone who witnessed the amazing performance of 2,100 **representatives*** who attended the recent White House **Conference*** on Small Business would, I believe, agree that the entrepreneurial spirit in America is **on the verge of** making a new **breakthrough**.

Let me explain why.

First, and perhaps most important, small-business people have discovered that congressmen, senators, government officials—even the President of the U.S.—are willing, even anxious, to listen to them. This is true not only of the **delegates*** to the White House conference but of thousands, perhaps tens of thousands, of their friends who **got the word** when the delegates returned to their communities. Washington has finally heard how important they are to the future of the country. An **MIT** study completed last year by David L. Birch reported that small business is by far the largest **employer*** in the U.S. Of all new jobs in the U.S., 66% are generated by small businesses. A National Science Foundation study found that small companies **produce** 24 times as many innovations per research dollar as the largest.

MIT: Massachusetts Institute of Technology.
Employer: person who gives work for pay to others.
Produce: to make, manufacture, create.

Second, **vested interests** that have divided the **small-business community** in the past now have apparently been overcome. Two previous White House conferences—one in 1937, which ended in fist fights, and another in 1956, which ended in **platitudes**—were **failures***. A tremendous amount of planning went into the 1980 conference, but with the demanding voices of women, minorities, veterans, and other **factions**, this conference also could have ended in **clashes** and conflicts. Instead, to the amazement and delight of all participants, there was a spirit of **unanimity** and harmony, which clearly can establish the basis for a new and dynamic political voice.

Vested interests: strong concerns for something from which one expects benefit or advantage.
Small-business community: small business owners considered together.
Platitudes: attractive, appealing words that are nevertheless meaningless and trite.
Failures: not successes; not achieving desired results.
Factions: groups of persons forming a minority within a large group.
Clashes: disagreements.
Unanimity: unity of opinion.

Third, small-business people have now exchanged views on what they want to lobby for in the years ahead, and they have agreed on their **priorities**. The legislative **agenda*** for the next two years consists of 15 major **objectives*** agreed upon at the conference. They have been invited back to Washington to see how much they have been able to accomplish with the help of Congress and the Administration.

Priorities: what is believed to be more important.
Agenda: list of things to be done.
Objectives: goals, aims, targets.

The targets

Their 15 major **targets** fall into three groups.

Capital formation heads the list. Small-business men want **tax revisions** to encourage **continuity*** of family ownership and to provide tax-related **investment*** incentives. They want a **reduction*** in the amount of **paperwork*** necessary to take out an **SBA**-backed **loan***. Women want equal access to the SBA loan program.

Another group of objectives **calls on** the federal government to give **consideration*** to the small-business economy in creating economic **policy*** for the nation. They also want a review of all laws, regulations, and agencies that affect small business.

Finally, minorities and women want to be involved in the small business economy. Minorities are determined to make sure that laws already **on the books** that require setting aside a portion of federal **procurements*** for minority-owned businesses be strictly observed. Women entrepreneurs want **assistance*** in starting their own businesses and in taking advantage of various forms of management training. Their desire for practical training in business management is no different from that of the majority of business owners who wish to supplement their academic training with advice from small entrepreneurs who have personally experienced similar problems.

These are not **vague** generalizations. The small-business community has now developed a program to work toward their common

Targets: goals, aims.
Tax revisions: changes in tax law.
Continuity: the quality of going on without a break.
Investment: something bought for future income or benefit.
Reduction: lessening, diminishing, lowering.
Paperwork: written work (e.g., filling in forms, letter writing).
SBA: Small Business Administration.
Loan: money given for a certain period of time.
Calls on: here, requests.
Consideration: thinking about, taking into account.
Policy: guiding principle or procedure; course of action based on this.
On the books: currently in force, currently valid.
Procurements: something bought or acquired, as supplies.
Assistance: help, aid.

Vague: indefinite, unclear.

Small businesses, such as this one in New York City, may become politically powerful.

Political action committees: committees formed for the purpose of influencing governmental policies.

objectives. Regional groups such as COSIBA (Coalition of Small & Independent Business Assns.) and NSBA (National Small Business Assn.), among others, already are forming **political action committees** to influence local government policies. In addition, delegates from the conference have formed a committee that will create an organization in Washington to represent interests of small-business men and women from all over the country.

Reawakening: being made aware of again.

My own feeling is that the greatest impact of this new program may turn out to be the **reawakening*** of respect for, as well as the self-respect of, entrepreneurship in American life. Small-business people have considered themselves to be the unknown and forgotten little people of our economic system. They no longer believe this is true.

Proposals: suggestions, suggested plans.

What are the chances of new legislative action being taken as a result of the small-business lobby? How realistic are their **proposals***? There is no doubt that small-business people are politically important in America and their voices will be heard, but the results will depend, as they always do in political matters, on a balance among many competing ideas. However, a powerful political force will begin to exert its influence: The small-business people of the nation will have their say.

A warmer climate

One of the more remarkable consequences of this new element in American political life will be changing public attitudes toward business in general.

Lawmakers and the general public will have an inherent feeling of goodwill toward the corner storekeepers of America—the people who populate the Main Streets and shopping centers of every large and small city in the country. When these entrepreneurs speak about economic freedom, they will be respected by many of the **vociferous** critics who have long been convinced that big business is exploiting the public for its own gain. In fact, big business is going to find a new friend in those millions of small suppliers and customers.

Will big business support the political actions taken by the small-business community? Not all of them. For instance, big business may well have serious problems with small business's desire to increase the percentage of federal procurement funds set aside for small firms, as well as other issues. However, I anticipate that they will argue out their differences in a mutually sympathetic way and arrive at solutions that will, in my opinion, strengthen the whole economy.

Some people are still waiting for the curtain to fall on small business. I believe that the drama is just beginning and that the American way of life is due for a revival of spirit in the economic sphere as a direct result of the new determination of the small-business community to perform a starring role.

Vociferous: speaking loudly and noisily.

1. Business Vocabulary

A. Find the definitions of the following words. Put the letter of the word next to the definition.

a. entrepreneur	e. conference	i. proposal
b. investment	f. policy	j. paperwork
c. delegate	g. employer	k. objective
d. procurement	h. agenda	l. loan

——— 1. a person who starts a business and takes a risk for the profit

——— 2. a general principle laid down for the guidance of executives in handling their jobs

——— 3. a person or business that hires persons for wages or salary

——— 4. a list of things to be done

——— 5. money spent (capital) in order to gain a profit or interest

——— 6. a meeting for consultation or discussion

——— 7. work involving reports, letters, forms, etc.

——— 8. money lent for a period of time, bearing interest

——— 9. something purchased

——— 10. a plan which is suggested

——— 11. one who is authorized to act for or represent others

——— 12. a goal or aim

B. Complete the sentences with an appropriate form of the word in parentheses:

1. (awake)   Respect for small-business men and women will be _____ by this new program.

2. (continue)   Small-business owners want the government to help encourage _____ of family ownership.

3. (reduce)   Because SBA loans require a great deal of paperwork, the business owners want the amount of paperwork _____ .

4. (represent)   Over 2,100 people attended the White House Conference on Small Business as _____ .

5. (fail)   The two previous White House conferences in 1937 and 1956 were _____ .

6. (consider)   Among the objectives of the small-business owners is the desire that government should give _____ to the small-business economy.

7. (assist)   Among the many entrepreneurs who want governmental _____ are women.

2. Structural Review

A. Hypothetical situations in the past

A hypothetical situation in the past is one which did not happen, but is supposed or imagined.

> Example: If small-business people had organized earlier, they
> would have gained more attention from political leaders.

As in the above example, to indicate a hypothetical situation in the past, two clauses are joined. In one, *if* is used, plus *had*, plus a PAST PARTICIPLE, and in the other *would have* plus a PAST PARTICIPLE:

> (*If* . . . + *had* + PAST PARTICIPLE)
>
> (. . .*would* + *have* + PAST PARTICIPLE)

Complete the sentences with an appropriate form of the verb in parentheses.

1. There would have been no chance for new laws today if small-business people (consider) _____ themselves forgotten and unimportant.
2. If legislators had reviewed some of the older small-business laws earlier, per-haps they (throw) _____ them out.
3. The lobby (continue) _____ without any real voice if the entrepreneurial spirit (remain) _____ asleep.
4. The public (be) _____ less aware of the tremendous number of innova-tions which entrepreneurs produce if the National Science Foundation (support) _____ small-business research less.
5. If small-business men (define) _____ their needs earlier, they (express) _____ themselves more clearly.
6. Big business (continue) _____ to be the main concern of law makers if entrepreneurs (fail) _____ to speak out.
7. If the small-business community (develop) _____ a program to work toward common objectives, they (have) _____ a more forceful impact at the national level.
8. If the public (feel) _____ ill will toward entrepreneurs all these years, perhaps the recent reaction (be) _____ less positive.
9. If entrepreneurs (speak) _____ with a united voice earlier, perhaps leg-islators (question) _____ small-business tax laws more strongly.

B. Indirect Discourse

Review the explanation of indirect discourse presented in the *Structural Review* section of Chapter Eleven.

Revise the sentences below to eliminate *shifts* between indirect and direct dis-course by writing each sentence entirely in indirect discourse.

> Example: The businessman said, "The backbone of the
> American enterprise system *has* always been the
> ambitious entrepreneur" and that a businessman
> needed a good head for staying in the black.

Solution: The businessman said *that* the backbone of the American enterprise system *had* always been the ambitious entrepreneur and that a businessman needed a good head for staying in the black.

1. He noted, "The chief executive officer of the big corporation *has* had the loudest voice in regard to national economic policy," and that we would be hearing much more from the local businessmen.
2. He suggests, "This *is* not an overstatement" and that the entrepreneurial spirit in America was on the verge of making a breakthrough.
3. The article tells us that small-business people had discovered that governmental people would listen to them and, "Washington *has* finally heard how important they *are*."
4. The author feels, "The vested interests which *have* divided the small-business community in the past *have* been overcome" and that a spirit of unanimity and harmony was present.
5. The article reports, "Small-business people *have* exchanged views on what to lobby for in the future" and that they had agreed on their priorities.
6. We are told that the small-business men wanted tax revisions and, "Women *want* equal access to the SBA loan program."
7. Minorities and women said that they wanted to be involved in the small-business economy and, "*We are* determined to make sure that laws already on the books concerning federal procurements from minority-owned businesses be strictly observed."
8. The author said, "*My* own feeling *is* that the greatest impact of this new program could turn out to be the reawakening of respect for entrepreneurship" and that small-business people no longer believed they were the unknown and forgotten little people of the economic system.
9. The article concludes that large and small-business men would work together to strengthen the economy and "The American way of life *will* experience a re-awakening in the economic sphere as a result of the new determination of the small-business community."

Now write a one- to two-page memorandum to your supervisor, Mr. Jeremy Walsh, reporting on what the author of this article has said about the future prospects of small business in the United States. Use indirect discourse in reporting what the author said.

3. Business Communications

Writing policy statements

Chapter Thirteen has already mentioned policy statements as being guides to making decisions and conducting one's job. All large businesses have written policies, and they serve to provide guidance to employees, telling them exactly how they should conduct their work. Here, we shall discuss policies and learn how to write them.

Policies help standardize behavior in many decision-making situations by providing guidelines for action. For example, department stores want to keep their customers satisfied. These stores, therefore, may have a written policy which says that dissatisfied customers will be refunded their money on the cost of a purchase. Or, a university may have a policy that students, to be considered full-time students, must be enrolled for at least nine course hours each semester. If a student enrolls for only six course hours, the student is not considered a full-time student and will not be eligible for financial aid. One last example: many companies have a policy which states that the company first tries to fill new jobs with someone already within the company; if a person with the proper qualifications cannot be found within the company, only then will the company accept applications from people outside the company.

As you can see, policies such as these help managers make decisions more easily than if such policies did not exist. The department store clerk knows always to refund money to dissatisfied customers and does not need to ask a supervisor's permission to do so. A university knows whether a student is eligible for financial aid by the number of course hours the student is enrolled for. Lastly, a manager of a company automatically knows to search within the company whenever a job becomes open.

Because written policies help managers and employees make decisions and because this saves time, written policy statements are very common. They may be written when a new business, a new department, or a new job position is created. They may also be written to revise old, outdated policies. These policies may be on a variety of topics such as customer relations, sick leave, promotions in salaries, vacation time, and job performance.

When writing a policy, here are a few things to remember:

a. Be sure each policy statement discusses only one topic. Do not try, for example, to discuss sick leave and job performance in the same policy statement.

b. Be certain to include all necessary information such as who the policy concerns, what the topic of the policy is, when the policy applies, how the policy applies, and what the details of the policy are.

c. Write the policy statement in simple language. Try to use short sentences and simple words.

d. Be sure the tone of the statement is either pleasant or factual. Do not write a policy in language that might make someone angry. Do not use sexist language.

Sexist: An employee will be promoted
                 based on his ability, education, and
                 seniority.

Nonsexist: Employee promotions will be based
                 on ability, education, and seniority.

An example of a policy statement follows.

Sick Leave
    As an employee of X company you are
allowed time off with pay when, because of
illness, you are not able to work. Pay for

sick leave is for the purpose of protecting
you against a possible loss of income due
to illness. You are allowed one paid sick
day per month. If you do not use all of
your sick leave days within a year, you
may add the days you do not use to the
next year's total. A maximum of thirty
days paid sick leave may be accumulated.

Now, try writing a policy statement for each of the following topics:

> coffee breaks
> vacations
> salary increases
> employee absences
> terminating employees

4. Action

Panel discussion

The local chapter of the National Small Business Association is interested in informing entrepreneurs about the possibilities for influencing legislation on the state and national level and persuading them to join the organization and to cooperate in the effort. For this purpose an open meeting has been called and several members of the political action committee of the local NSBA chapter have agreed to appear on a panel.

Divide the class into small groups. Each student should take the role of one of the panel members.

The panel will include the owner of a local supermarket, the son of a jeweler with a family-run business, the owner of a print shop (a woman), a car dealer (a black), as well as a state legislator who desires to assure the small-business people that government wants to hear about their problems. Use your imagination to create other panel members to adjust the size of the panel group to the needs of your class. Each member of the panel should review the article to prepare his own brief statement for the audience and be prepared to enter into a general discussion once the individual presentations have been made.

5. Reaction

Questions for discussion

1. How have the small-business men and women organized themselves into a powerful political group? In your country, do people organize themselves this way? In what way do people influence the government in your country?
2. Can you suggest any reasons why respect for entrepreneurship has declined in the past? Why is this respect beginning to reawaken? Would this reawakening

have begun if the business people had not organized themselves into a politically active group?

3. Do you think big business will find a "new friend" in these small businesses? Will the goals and business procedures of big business be the same as those of small business owners? How much competition can small business give big business?

4. Are the predictions in this article correct? Will small business actually become a strong force in the political and economic life of America? The article concerns something that has not yet happened. The writer always speaks of the future, such as: "about to become the most powerful political lobby in the country," and "we will be hearing much more from the collective voice of the local florist," and "the small-business people of the nation will have their say." Is his optimism justified?

CHAPTER FOURTEEN: Who Gets Promoted?

Alfred W. Swinyard and Floyd A. Bond   *Harvard Business Review*

Vantage point: point of view, manner of thinking.

*Every corporate manager who has reached the top has his or her opinions about the competition; depending on **vantage point**, such managers see their competition as older, younger, much smarter, or "not quite up to snuff." But we know of no recent research effort that clears up the controversy about who gets promoted or that separates fact from biased generalizations. In this article, the authors depict the "new breed" of top manager, a picture they are eminently qualified to draw after studying for ten full years the characteristics and backgrounds of the newly promoted executives.*

Survey: a general or comprehensive study.

Predecessors: persons or things which came before another.
Peers: those equal in rank, position, or quality.
Advanced degrees: ranks or grades given by a university beyond the bachelor's degree (which is normally completed in four years of study).
Forebears: predecessors, those who have gone before.
Group vice presidents: vice presidents in charge of several branches or sections of the company.
Senior vice president: generally a prestige title indicating a top vice president with top executive responsibilities.
Executive vice president: vice president with decision-making powers just below the president.
Mobile: moving, able to be moved easily and quickly, especially from company to company.

Here are some of the important trends we discovered in a **survey** of more than 11,000 executives taken at the time they were promoted to vice president or president of a major U.S. company:

● New entrants into the ranks of U.S. top management are better educated than their **predecessors*** and their nonbusiness **peers***.

● The largest percentage of advanced degrees are held in business administration (**advanced degrees*** in law and engineering are next most prevalent).

● At the same time, the newly promoted executives are not likely to be any younger than their **forebears** when they "make the grade."

● Those who reach the level of president in their organizations will most likely have been **group vice presidents*** (not **senior*** or **executive vice presidents***) chosen from inside the company, and they will probably not have spent more than four years in their previous positions.

● Top executives now tend to be more **mobile*** because of changes in promotional patterns and in their own opportunities. This

148

tendency is increasing and may prove beneficial in the long run, given the superior educational backgrounds and more diversified business experiences of the candidates.

These findings come from our research on high-level executives promoted during the period 1967 through 1976. Our research effort's main purpose was to identify the character of a new, seemingly younger **breed** of top manager, about whom **exceedingly** little has been written. What we discovered is reassuring and **reinforces** the overall impression that, as a whole, American business people are now better informed and more sophisticated—just at the time they most need to be.

Breed: kind or sort.
Exceedingly: extremely, very greatly.
Reinforces: strengthens, supports.

Better educated at the top

The newly promoted executive is indeed well educated. More than ever before, he or she is certain to have gone to college and, increasingly, to graduate school. In fact, as a group, the executives in our study have more formal education than either the general population or their college peers.

In contrast, the percentage of executives completing only a bachelor's degree remained relatively constant. Law degree recipients also made up about the same portion in 1976 as in 1967, but the percentage reporting other advanced degrees (such as PhDs or MDs) increased slightly. In total, the proportion of graduate degrees increased from 33% in 1967 to 41% in 1976. (See *Exhibit I*.)

Exhibit I
Highest degree obtained (1967 and 1976)

Highest degree	Percentage of executives	
	1967	1976
High school graduate or less	6%	3%
Some college education	12	8
Bachelor's degree	49	48
Master's degree	18	25
Law degree	12	11
Doctorate (PhD, MD, etc.)	3	5

Specific fields of interest

The information about our executives' undergraduate education shows that their most common **field of study*** was business administration (27%), followed closely by engineering (26%), and social and **behavioral science**—including economics (22%). Fully 42% of those with undergraduate degrees went on to the graduate level.

Graduate degrees in business administration and management

Field of study: topic, subject, or area of academic interest or specialization.
Behavioral science: a science, such as psychology or sociology, which investigates social activity.

Exhibit II
Area of highest degree of newly promoted executives (1967 and 1976)

Area of highest degree	Percentage of executives 1967	1976
Business administration	22%	33%
Engineering	22	18
Law	12	11
Mathematics & science	8	6
Economics	6	6
Social & behavioral science (excluding economics)	3	5
All other	7	6
N.A. by field	2	4
No degree	18	11

Textiles: cloth, fabrics.

attracted the largest portion of our sample group. The percentage of newly promoted executives who reported their highest degree in business administration increased dramatically between 1967 and 1976. (See *Exhibit II.*) Among those with bachelor's degrees in business administration who did graduate work, two-thirds achieved a master's degree in the same field, while one-third secured a law degree.

A summary of the educational choices of executives earning graduate degrees shows that 45% chose business administration as their major field. Law was the second choice, followed by engineering. (It is interesting to note that nearly 25% of the newly promoted executives with law degrees also had undergraduate degrees in business administration.)

When separating the data by industry, we discovered some variations on the theme. Fully 33 industries (with at least 200 executives in each one) are represented by our group. But in only 14 of them did more than 40% report graduate degrees; the leaders include pharmaceuticals, real estate and land development (the field with the highest percentage of lawyers), investment banking, communications, chemicals, printing and publishing, and electronics and electronic products. Industries with less than 30% of the executives reporting graduate degrees included apparel, **textiles**, and construction.

Succession: the sequence in which one person after another gets a certain job.
Refute: say something is wrong, contradict.
Contention: a statement made as part of an argument in favor of a point of view.

The impact of age on management *succession**

Just as professors insist that students get younger every year, many older executives claim that the "up and coming" types are appointed at steadily younger ages. Our data, however, **refute** this **contention**. In fact, the median age of the newly promoted executives in

1967, in 1976, and for the ten-year period as a whole was 47. Slight variations occurred from year to year, but the age of the entire group remained relatively constant.

However, there are definite variations on the basis of executive position. The age of presidents who were also CEOs* varied only slightly on an annual basis, **hovering** around 47. But presidents who were not CEOs had a median age of 49, and presidents of subsidiaries, divisions, or groups had a median age of 46.

Hovering: remaining, staying (near something).

Future career *prospects*

One part of the **questionnaire shed** some **light** on future career prospects for the executives in our sample. We asked more than 6,000 vice presidents to report the age of their companies' presidents. The median age turned out to be 54, with 26% between the ages of 56 and 60, and with 13% who were 61 or older.

Prospects: possibilities, eventualities, possible future events.
Questionnaire: a list of questions for a survey.
Shed light: illuminated, enlightened, made clear.

If we consider retirement age to be 65, we could reasonably **postulate** that 13% of these presidents would have to be replaced within five years, and nearly 40% within ten. But if we also assume that more than five years' service is required for any executive to be considered a **candidate*** for president, we see that almost 42% of the newly promoted vice presidents would be too old to get the job.

Postulate: suppose, assume, hypothesize.
Candidate: person seeking or nominated for a position.

Further, the future is markedly less promising for executive and senior vice presidents (who are usually the same age as or less than five years younger than their presidents) than for group vice presidents. (See *Exhibit III*.) That leaves about 55% of the group vice

Exhibit III
Age relationship of newly promoted vice presidents to their presidents

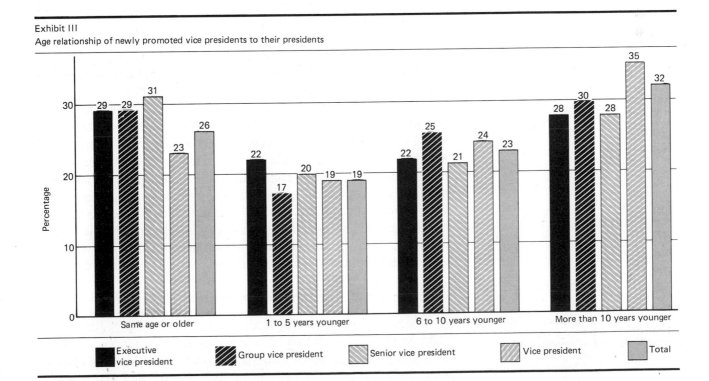

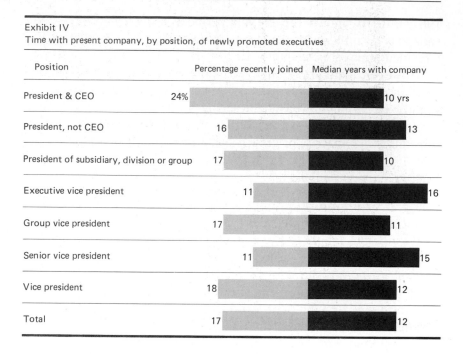

Exhibit IV
Time with present company, by position, of newly promoted executives

Position	Percentage recently joined	Median years with company
President & CEO	24%	10 yrs
President, not CEO	16	13
President of subsidiary, division or group	17	10
Executive vice president	11	16
Group vice president	17	11
Senior vice president	11	15
Vice president	18	12
Total	17	12

presidents as logical candidates for promotion to the presidency of their companies.

What they did before

Two aspects of the executives' career experiences are noteworthy: length of time spent with their present companies and nature of their previous positions—including how much time they spent in that position. The first aspect is shown in *Exhibit IV*.

In most cases, presidents reported they had a fairly long history with their companies. The presidents who were also CEOs reported that they had recently joined their companies in 24% of the cases, and they had the shortest median period of service—ten years. The percentage of other executives who had joined recently was lower, only 11% of executive and senior vice presidents. Executive vice presidents had the longest median period of service—16 years. For the total group over the decade, only 17% had recently joined their companies. Twelve years was the median length of service for all executives.

Before becoming president, an executive generally varies position often within the company. Although they may have spent a considerable amount of time in the organization, 59% of our executives had held their previous positions for less than four years—with a median of 3.4 years.

Prior experience varies

Our executives' previous experience ranged from general management (here considered to include **operations management*, divi-**

Prior: former, before.
Operations management: management function related to design, implementation, and control of human/machine systems required to produce a given produce or service.

sion management*, and administration) to functional areas (finance, marketing, manufacturing, **corporate planning***, and other activities). The four most common areas reported were operations (36%), finance (18%), and administration and marketing (both at 15%). Only 5% of the executives reported prior experience in corporate planning.

When we look at previous experience along position lines, we see that certain positions seem to **link** up with certain kinds of experience. Previous experience in operations or division management **ranked** first in all positions and was reported by 43% to 65% of the group vice presidents and three types of presidents. Finance was a strong second among executive vice presidents and senior vice presidents, while marketing was in second position among the presidents of subsidiaries, divisions, or groups.

Our study suggests something else: the average marketing executive may no longer have the **requisite** educational background to reach the top. Patterns among more than 6,000 vice presidents in our sample show that only 17% of the marketing vice presidents had **MBA** degrees, compared with 30% of the finance and accounting vice presidents. The data can be looked at in another way— 21% of the marketing vice presidents had no college degree, in contrast to only 8% without a bachelor's for those in finance or accounting.

Educational background and age

Younger executives pushing into the ranks of top management are generally better educated than their predecessors. *Exhibit V* plots

Division management: administration and guidance of a subordinate administrative unit of an organization, bureau, or agency.
Corporate planning: a systematic, step-by-step method of defining, developing, and outlining possible courses of action to meet existing or future needs of the corporation.

To link: to connect, to join.
Ranked: placed in a row or in sequence or order.

Requisite: required, necessary.
MBA: master's degree in business administration.

Exhibit V
Age, by educational background, of newly promoted executives

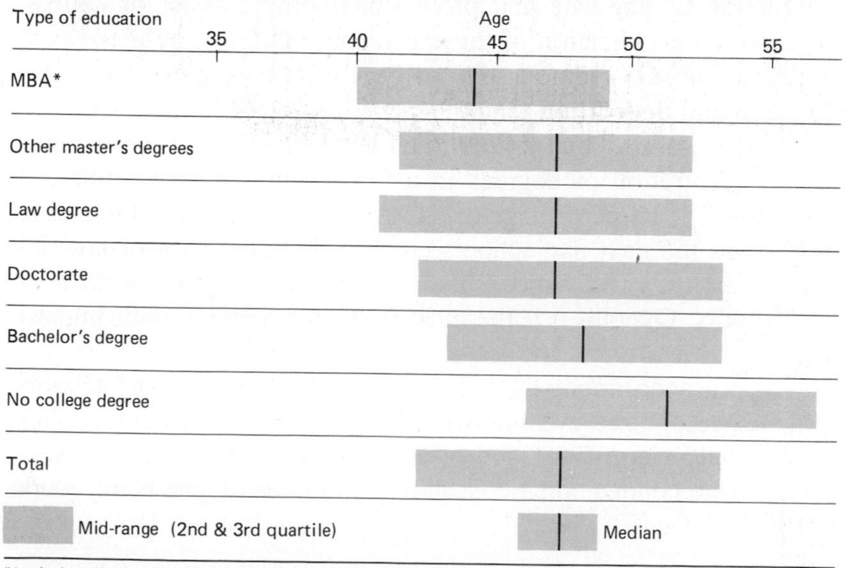

*Includes all master's degrees (MBA and others) in business administration. The MBA represents more than 90% of the group.

Differentials: differences, amount of differences.

the median age of the newly promoted manager by type of educational background rather than position. This exhibit also suggests that an executive with an MBA does have a clearer road to the top at an earlier age.

Newly promoted executives with MBA degrees had a median age of 44, whereas executives with other types of graduate education—such as a master's degree in another discipline or a law, doctoral, or medical degree—had a median age of 47. Executives with only a bachelor's degree had a median age of 48, while those without a college degree had a median age of 51. The median age **differentials** show executives with MBA degrees moving up more quickly.

According to the survey, executives with advanced degrees are well represented at all levels of the top executive family. A slightly higher percentage (up to 35%) of the older executive groups are presidents, and it is these groups that have less education. More important, these older groups with less formal education have fewer vice presidents among them, and we can expect that the normal course of management succession will continue to reduce the number in top executive ranks.

Accelerating: increasing in speed, speeding up.

Current evidence indicates that these education-linked promotion trends are, in fact, **accelerating***. Already in the beginning of the 1980s, about 25% of all newly promoted top executives hold MBA degrees—representing a 39% increase over the average for the decade covered by our study.

Are old school *ties* important?

Ties: links, connections; also used as applying to "old school neckties."
Dedication: commitment, singleness of purpose.

Surveys of executive characteristics sometimes concentrate on the known facts of education and experience and forget the importance of such personal attributes as determination and ambition. But the completion of graduate and professional programs is, of course, one important indication of these personal qualities, as is the type of school chosen—some traditionally require more personal determination and **dedication** than others.

On the graduate and professional level, there is a more significant concentration of degrees in a few leading schools. Harvard heads the list. Its percentage of master's degrees awarded is nearly as large as the next five schools combined. In the case of law degrees, Harvard's 15% exceeds the combined percentages of the next two schools. Overall, it is the most frequent source of their highest degree.

Urban: of or in a town or city.
Goal orientation: concern with finishing a job or achieving an objective.
Perseverance: determination, staying power, firmness of purpose.

The presence among the leaders of several large **urban*** schools with well-recognized evening MBA programs is significant. It points up the **goal orientation*** and **perseverance** shown by some executives—who continue their educational programs despite heavy work loads.

A summary of trends

While the results of our study tend to **fall in line** with generally recognized historical trends, they underscore the necessity for adjustments both in our educational system and in our way of thinking about managers. Because the changes taking place were so rapid, we were able to see them clearly in a single decade. We have come to the conclusion that institutions—and commonly held opinions—are not adjusting with the same rapidity.

The most obvious change is in educational background; there is a marked increase in graduate and professional education among corporate executives, a decrease in the number of those without college degrees, and a continuing rise in the importance attached to the master's degree in business administration.

Business administration will continue to hold its position as the major career choice of entering college students, particularly women, while traditional fields, such as education and science, decline. Our educational systems must adjust to the change both by continuing to upgrade the quality of education for business administration and by making it more readily available.

Besides this educational "**uplifting**," the other change we note is the increasing mobility of top executives. We expect a substantial proportion of highly qualified executives to be blocked from promotion for various reasons (either they will have advanced to a certain level at too young an age, will have been shifted to a senior or executive vice presidential position from which it will be difficult to leave, or will have fallen in the competition with their equally well-educated peers).

Any of these reasons could lead directly to a desire to change companies or to transfer within the management system. (The new mobility is already **making its mark**—reportedly there were more than 2,000 **executive search organizations*** at the end of 1979.) We feel, however, that the high degree of mobility will not result in **chaos**; the executives will not only have superior educational backgrounds but will also have extremely diversified business experiences.

To fall in line: to agree, to be consistent.

Uplifting: increase in quality, upgrading.

Making its mark: becoming significant or important.
Executive search organizations: businesses whose function is placing management-level candidates in jobs.
Chaos: complete disorder.

1. Business Vocabulary

A.   Fill in the blanks in the letter below with a word or words from the list provided. Each word or term is to be used only one time.

succession	candidate	accelerates
executive search	goal oriented	advanced degrees
organization	peers	fields of study
predecessors	mobile	urban

April 15, 19– –

John B. Blake
Professor of Marketing
Edward's College
Carmel, N.H. 10320

Mr. Roy J. Butler
President
Association of Professional Marketing Managers
123 W. First Street, NW
Boise, Idaho 11320

Dear Mr. Butler:

After reading a recent article in the *Harvard Business Review*, I am concerned for my _____ and myself as marketing managers and executives.

The article indicated that those executives who hold certain _____, especially the MBA, are more likely to be promoted to the higher executive levels. This, of course, depends on where one received his degree. Some of the _____ night schools have good reputations, and this helps when one becomes a _____ for advancement. At any rate, education is more important now than it was for our _____, and among the possible _____, marketing seems to be one from which few people are advancing.

Do you have any thoughts on why this is happening? The study found that only 17% of the marketing vice-presidents had MBA degrees; does this mean that as a group we have less diversified business experiences? I wonder if we stay with one job for too many years and thereby become less _____? Mobility seems to be important now. I do not think we are any less _____ than are our peers.

As this trend of not promoting marketing specialists _____, the process of management _____ will continue to include fewer and fewer people from our profession. I am concerned about this trend and wonder if the Association can work toward any meaningful resolution of the problem. Perhaps we could develop within the Association an _____ _____ _____. This is only one possibility.

I am sure you share my concerns, and I look forward to discussing this issue with you in the near future.

Sincerely,

John B. Blake

B. Find the definitions of the following terms. Put the letter of the term next to the definition.

a. executive vice president
b. division management
c. group vice president

d. senior vice president
e. CEO
f. corporate planning
g. operations management

_____ 1. Person with total responsibility for all decision making in the corporation

_____ 2. High executive office with a title sometimes felt to have special prestige

_____ 3. Administration of a company branch or section

_____ 4. Aspect of management including systematic consideration of planning, problem solving, forecasting, and decision making

_____ 5. Vice president in charge of one part of the company

_____ 6. A vice president with general decision-making responsibility directly under the president

_____ 7. The systematic work of forecasting and taking into account corporate responsibilities

2. Structural Review

Comparison

The *comparative* form of adjectives and adverbs is used to compare two persons or items, and the *superlative* form to compare three or more.

Comparative: (1) ADJ + -er   ADV + -er
                   (cheaper)   *(faster)*
              (2) *more* + ADJ   *more* + ADV
                   (more economical)   *(more rapidly)*

Superlative: (1) ADJ + -est   ADV + -est
                   (cheapest)   *(fastest)*
              (2) *most* + ADJ   *most* + ADV
                   (most economical)   *(most rapidly)*

Generally, one- or two-syllable words add -*er* to form the comparative and -*est* to form the superlative, but there is no perfect rule. Many adjectives and adverbs can add -*er* and -*est* or, on the other hand, *more* and *most*. Both forms are thus frequently equally correct.

When the standard is *not* cited in the sentence (that is, the *than* clause, for example, taller *than Bill*), the superlative is usually used instead of the comparative in American business English, whereas in Standard English this usage is still often considered informal.

Example: Dr. Albright is the *more capable* of the two managers.
            or,
            Dr. Albright is the *most capable* of the two managers.
But: Dr. Albright is *more capable than* the senior vice president.

The form or EQUATION is *as . . . as*:

Example: Johnson is *as* goal oriented *as* Murchison.

The form for expressing INFERIORITY is *less . . . than*:

Example: French high-level executives are *less* mobile *than* their American counterparts.

Choose from among the following comparative and superlative expressions to fill in the blanks. Familiarity with the article will help you to complete the sentences correctly. Each word or phrase is used one time.

most frequent	better	largest
clearer	most	more
younger	more than	less
more readily	highest	

1. New entrants into the ranks of top management are _____ educated than their predecessors.
2. The _____ degrees which most newly promoted executives had achieved were in the fields of business administration and management.
3. Those who reach the level of president in their organizations will _____ likely have been group vice presidents, and they will probably have spent _____ than four years in their previous positions.
4. Our research effort's main purpose was to identify the character of a new, _____ breed of top manager.
5. For promotions to vice president or to president, the _____ percentage of advanced degrees are held in business administration.
6. Although they may have spent a considerable amount of time in the organization, 59% of executives had held their previous positions for _____ than four years—with a median of 3.4 years.
7. The MBA, it seems, does have a _____ road to the top than his competition with no such degree.
8. Overall, Harvard is the _____ source of executives' highest degrees.
9. Our educational systems must upgrade the quality of education for business administration and make it _____ available.
10. Reportedly there were _____ 2,000 executive search organizations at the end of 1979.

3. Business Communications

Abstracts

Like a summary, an abstract is a short description or condensation of a piece of writing. It is usually found at the beginning of long reports, or before articles in professional journals with the special purpose of saving the reader time. Abstracts are usually a page or less in length and are most often in the form of one paragraph.

The purpose of the abstract, then, is to inform the reader briefly and concisely of the problem considered in the paper; the scope or extent of the study presented; and the paper's findings, conclusions, and the recommendations so that the reader may know whether he is interested enough to read it or if there are certain parts that interest him more than others. If there are, he can spend his time reading the parts particularly important for his purposes.

An abstract begins by explaining the main topic that the paper considers and why it needs study. Then it gives the scope of the study (how far and how deep does the study go?). Many problems are broad, and the report may only consider one part of a larger problem. For example, changes in the social security system may have both economic and social aspects, and a report may consider only the social side of the problem. Finally, the abstract states what the study found, what conclusions are drawn from these findings, and what recommendations are made based on these conclusions.

Stylistically, abstracts make frequent use of the passive voice (*It was found that . . .*) and of indirect discourse (*He said that . . .*).

In summary, an abstract is a particular kind of summary written for the purpose of explaining the basic points of a study (like the report from *Harvard Business Review* in this chapter). Ordinarily, only studies are "abstracted," whereas other forms of writing, like news stories, are "summarized."

ABSTRACT

Problem:	The issue is raised of the businessman's inability to write well. It is reported that executives find the quality of written reports, letters, and memos has been de-
Scope:	teriorating. Discussion is presented of a few representative businesses which have sought to correct the problem by re-educating their employees through commercial report writing courses. It is reported
Findings:	that executives have found that, as a result of such training, less time is spent reading and writing reports, the points being made can be more easily grasped, and
Conclusions:	excessive verbiage can be eliminated. Such retraining may be only marginally effective until writing schools and instructors
Recommendation:	change their methods, yet many businesses may find themselves in a position to benefit from such courses.

The article in this chapter reports the results of a study conducted by the author. Using the information given in the article, abstract the study as reported.

4. Action

Informal class debate

Divide the class into two teams to debate informally the qualifications needed for executives:

Team A: Modern candidates for a corporate presidency should have a graduate degree in business or a related field (preferably an MBA), should have a wide variety of professional experiences with several corporations, and should not be over 50 years of age. Education, mobility (and thus flexibility), diversity of experience, and youthfulness are necessary qualities. These qualities reflect the needs of modern business.

Team B: Modern business is no different than business has always been. Sound executive-level judgment still requires that a person have many years of professional experience within his industry and within his corporation. Years of experience are more important than a graduate degree in business. Having mobility and diversity of experience are not, then, as important as having lengthy experience within the industry and corporation. At the presidential level, the lack of experience and understanding of the young are undesirable.

Allow each team five to seven minutes of group preparation followed by a three-minute presentation (timed with a watch). Allow time for a rebuttal of three minutes by each team.

5. Reaction

Questions for discussion

1. The article points out that here is a "new mobility . . . already making its mark" among executives in the United States. The authors feel that this mobility will not have negative results, but rather that the executives will have an "extremely diversified business experience." In other nations, such as Japan, mobility is not acceptable. Can you explain why two highly industrialized nations have two very different opinions about the mobility of management? Consider which quality companies consider more important: loyalty or variety of experience. Which of these two is more important in your country? How mobile are executives in your country?

2. Why might industries like apparel, textiles, and construction have fewer executives with graduate degrees than other industries like real estate, investment banking, communications, chemicals, and electronics?

3. The study reported in this article indicates that executives who become president of a company have usually "spent a considerable amount of time in the organization." The study reveals, however, that 59% of these presidents had held their previous positions for less than "four years—with a median of 3.4 years." This may indicate that executives who find themselves in a lower-level position for more than four years have less chance of advancement within their company, especially to the position of president. What should an executive, a vice-president of sales for example, do when he finds himself in the same position for six years? Should he consider moving to another company? Does the fact that he has been in the same position for more than four years mean that he will not advance further within the company?

4. The schools reported in this study are all prestigious. Admission to and graduation from these schools requires a great deal of perseverance and goal orientation. Which do you think is more important to advancement in executive-level work, the name of the school on the diploma, or the fact that you are a determined and hard-working person? What are the nonacademic advantages of attending a prestigious school?

5. The information presented from the survey is factual and little evaluation of promotional policies is attempted. What are the advantages and disadvantages of the current promotional policies in the U.S.? How would you change them if you were to use them to create policies in your own company?

CHAPTER FIFTEEN: **Those Business Hunches* That Pay**

Roy Rowan *Fortune*

Hunches: definite feelings that something may be true.

A beauty: very fine (informal).
Cost analysis: study of potential costs for a project.
On the money: very accurate (informal).
Sales projections: estimated amount of sales.
Pie-in-the-sky: wishful, hopeful, rather than accurate (informal).
Nagging: complaining constantly.
Hold off on: postpone, wait until later for (informal).
Subordinates: persons working under another.
Disguise: hide or cover up the true appearance.
Gut: seeming to originate from body feelings, not from the mind.

Psychic: of mental processes beyond the five senses.
Academicians: persons whose profession is in teaching or scholarly study.
Subconscious: below the normal areas of mental awareness.
Heeding: paying attention to, responding to.

Odious: hateful, very distasteful, disgusting.
Imprecision: lack of accuracy.
Precognitive: knowing in advance of the event itself.
Occult: magic, having to do with the powers of darkness.
Shrinks from: withdraws from suddenly, jerks away from.
Kooks: crazy persons (informal).

The feasibility study is **a beauty**. The **cost analysis*** looks right **on the money**. Even the **sales projections***, sometimes a little **pie-in-the-sky,** seem pretty solid. All the ingredients needed for a sound decision say: "Go!" Yet this **nagging** voice from deep inside his brain keeps repeating: "No!"

"Let's **hold off on** this one," announces the CEO to his astonished **subordinates***.

Weak excuses like that cannot **disguise*** the fact that most of the chief executives who control the biggest corporations are often guided by ill-defined **gut** feelings.

When biology feeds back

Society's current addiction to **psychic** advice is hardly what executives mean when they admit to following hunches.

Yet, a handful of scientists and **academicians*** have come up with measurable proof that **subconscious** elements play a role in the decision-making process. They are convinced that **heeding** a strong hunch may be wise. They point out that it isn't realistic for executives to rely solely on logic to cope with the complexities of modern business.

Mention these thoughts to a board chairman or president, and you had better watch your language. To begin with, hunch is an **odious** word to the professional manager. It's a term full of **imprecision** and unpredictability. *Psychic* and **precognitive** are just as bad, since they imply the **occult**. The business leader understandably **shrinks from** the thought of being associated with such **kooks**.

But suggest to this same executive that he might indeed possess certain **intuitive*** powers, which could be of assistance in generating ideas, choosing alternative courses of actions, and picking people, and you'll get some interesting responses:

"The chief executive officer is not supposed to say, 'I feel.' He's supposed to say 'I know,'" asserts David Mahoney, chairman of Norton Simon. "So we **deify** the word **instinct*** by calling it judgment. But any attempt to deny instinct is to deny identity. It's the most current thing. It's me—in everything from picking a wife to picking a company for **acquisition***."

"In a business that depends entirely on people and not machinery," says Robert Bernstein, chairman of Random House, "only intuition can protect you against the most dangerous individual of all—the **articulate incompetent***. That's what frightens me about business schools. They train their students to sound wonderful. But it's necessary to find out if there's judgment behind the language."

"Physics is all hunches and intuition," admits Herman Kahn, a trained physicist-turned-futurist and now director of the Hudson Institute. "My research is a combination of intuition and judgment. I don't know where it comes from. The mind simply puts things together."

Are you *fortune's darling?*

As Max Gunther points out in *The Luck Factor*: "The facts on which the hunch is based are stored and processed on some level of awareness just below the conscious level. This is why the hunch comes with that **peculiar** feeling of almost-but-not-quite knowing." But Gunther, an author of books on human relations, also warns against **disregarding** those "odd little hunches that are trying to tell you what you don't want to hear. Never assume you are fortune's darling." Failure to maintain some degree of pessimism, he claims, is to be in a state of **peril**.

There are other warnings that the **wily** manager should heed: never confuse hope with a hunch, and never regard a hunch as a substitute for first acquiring all known data (laziness usually produces **lousy** hunches). However, since management itself is an inexact science—frequently defined as the "art of making decisions with insufficient information"—even the most deliberate CEO may be forced to act **prematurely** on an inner impression.

Possibly, then, it is in matters of timing that the business hunch is most important, as Robert P. Jensen, chairman of General Cable Corp., will **testify**. Last year, sensing the need for his company to diversify, he found himself faced with five major decisions that involved $300 million in sell-offs and acquisitions. "On each decision," says Jensen, "the mathematical analysis only got me to the point where my intuition had to **take over**"—as was the case with the $106-million cash purchase of Automation Industries.

An engineer not given to **precipitate** decisions, he calls "patience" crucial to the intuitive process. "It's easy to step in and say

Intuitive: knowing without thinking logically.

Deify: make a god of.
Instinct: inborn impulse, intuition, or behavior.
Acquisition: something bought or otherwise gained or obtained.

Articulate: able to speak well.
Incompetent: not capable of doing one's job.

Fortune: fate, luck, destiny, chance.
Darling: favorite, preferred.
Peculiar: strange; special.
Disregarding: not paying attention to, ignoring.
Peril: great danger.

Wily: clever, tricky.
Lousy: very bad, disgusting (very informal).
Prematurely: before the right time.

Testify: state or witness as in a court of law.
To take over: to take command, to take control.

Precipitate: very quick.

Weigh in with: contribute to a discussion.
Move: action, act (informal).

I have a feeling we ought to do this or that. But then you haven't let your managers **weigh in with** their feelings first." At the same time, he warns that the perfectionist who keeps waiting for new information never gets anything done. "Intuition is picking the right moment for making your **move**," adds Jensen, who spent three years as a tight end for the Baltimore Colts.

Reveling in "*calculated* chaos"

Reveling: taking intense joy or delight in something, being extremely happy.
Calculated: carefully thought out.
Evidence: information on which a conclusion may be based.

There is, in fact, considerable **evidence*** that the rational CEO is a fiction. That, anyway, is the view of Professor Henry Mintzberg of the McGill University Faculty of Management, who has been studying and writing about the executive for a dozen years.

Systematic: organized, logical and well-planned.
Holistic: taken as a whole, not to be considered as a collection of parts.
Portrays: gives a picture of, draws.
Unrelenting: without giving up, unyielding, without stopping or slowing.
Rational: logical, reasonable.

According to Mintzberg, the CEO pays little real attention to **systematic*** long-range planning, tables of organization, and reliance on computers and quantitative techniques. In reality he's a "**holistic**, intuitive thinker who revels in a climate of calculated chaos." Mintzberg **portrays** the CEO as working at an **unrelenting** pace, jumping from topic to topic, disposing of items in ten minutes or less, and "constantly relying on hunches to cope with problems far too complex for **rational** analysis."

Linear: sequential, logical, rational.
Spatial: having to do with space and arrangements.

This ability to absorb all manner of information stems from the fact that chief executives seem to be "right-brain dominated." It was long known that the right side of the brain controls the left side of the body—and vice versa. Only recently, however, was it discovered that the two sides of the brain seem to specialize in different activities. The left appears to handle the logical, **linear**, verbal functions. The right takes care of the emotional, intuitive, **spatial** functions.

Electroencephalograph: device for measuring electronic impulses from the brain.
Relied on: depended on with confidence, looked to for help.

To confirm this application of the right-brain, left-brain theory to business, Robert Doktor, a University of Hawaii business-school professor, wired up a number of CEOs to an **electroencephalograph** to find out which side of the brain they **relied on*** most. The right side won.

Intangibles: that which cannot be felt or sensed.
Infer: draw conclusions from evidence.

It was only a question of time before word of the right-brained boss would leak out and somebody would develop a market for the "soft information"—gossip, clues, insights, and other **intangibles**—on which the intuitive mind feeds. **Infer**-mation, as the Williams Inference Service of New York calls itself, now sells educated hunches ("disciplined intuition" is the term it uses) to companies such as Travelers and IU International.

A *masquerade* of memories

Masquerade: a party at which masks are worn; a disguise.
Ingenious: brilliant, unique.

In today's unpredictable environment, it's hard to tell whether even the "best" hunches will work. A CEO may come up with an **ingenious*** concept that he can't sell. Aware that universities were concerned about the "social content of their investments," Howard Stein, chairman of Dreyfus Corp., launched a special mutual fund* in

Philippe Weisbecker

1972 composed only of companies that strictly complied with environmental **safeguards*** and **fair-employment practices***. "Ironically, this Third Century Fund has outperformed most others," reports Stein, "but the colleges called it a '**do-good** attempt' and stuck to traditional investments."

In addition, William F. May, chairman of American Can Co., warns that "you have to be alert not to let bad memories masquerade as intuition." He cites his company's experience with the two-quart milk container, which failed miserably when it was first introduced in 1934. The company **revived** the idea in 1955 in the belief

Safeguards: conditions that give protection.
Fair-employment practices: equal consideration of all job applicants and workers, without bias or prejudice.
Do-good: too nice, falsely or hypocritically doing good for others (informal).

Revived: gave life to again.

Turned down: refused, said no to.

that its time had come. "Our executives **turned** it **down**," says May. Today, American Can's competitors have two-quart containers in every dairy case.

Precognition and profits

To decipher: to decode, to make understandable.
ESP: extrasensory perception.

This ability to **decipher** the signs of the future puts an enormous premium on what the parapsychologists (**ESP** specialists) call "precognition." Almost two decades of testing executives have uncovered a close link between a CEO's precognitive and profit-making abilities. In research conducted at the New Jersey Institute of Technology, engineer John Mihalasky and parapsychologist E. Douglas Dean found that more than 80 percent of CEOs who had doubled their company's profits within a five-year period proved to have above-average precognitive powers.

Guts: intestines, courage.
Unique: one of a kind.

"If something goes beyond the logic that we understand," cautions Mihalasky, "we say forget it." In any case, "the biggest roadblock to intuitive decision-making is not having the **guts** to follow a good hunch." He offers certain recommendations for inducing intuition: (1) Concentrate on what is **unique**. (2) Be aware of the gaps in your knowledge. (3) Make connections between diverse factors. (4) Avoid becoming overloaded with information.

Indebtedness: state of owing money; amount of money owed.

While executives may hide the importance of the hunch, non-business leaders are not so reluctant to acknowledge their **indebtedness*** to it. Helen Gurley Brown confides that she uses "secret personal knowledge" in editing *Cosmopolitan*. "When I read a manuscript, even if it's not well written, only intuition can say this is truth, readers will like it. Or intuition may tell me that a piece by a Pulitzer prizewinner is a phony."

Deductive: here, logical.
Assault: attack.

Artists, certainly, always assumed that creativity doesn't spring from a **deductive assault** on a problem. Yet there are instances where a joining of the intuitive and deductive helped them produce magnificent results. From Leonardo da Vinci's pen came detailed drawings of the first flying machine. Both Robert Fulton, inventor of the steamboat, and Samuel Morse, inventor of the telegraph, started out life as artists. But intuition led them elsewhere.

Fervent: energetic, fanatic.
Evangelist: missionary, one who wishes to persuade others to a certain belief.

Today, it is an explorer back from outer space, Edgar Mitchell, who has turned into intuition's most **fervent evangelist**. A doctor of science from MIT, Navy captain, and the sixth man on the moon, he believes that "man's potential knowledge is more than the product of his five senses."

Founded: started, created, initiated (an organization, institution, etc.).
Computer software: written or printed, storable data, such as a computer program (not the computer itself or any of its parts).

Following that journey, Mitchell **founded** the Institute of Noetic Sciences (Greek for *intuitive knowing*) in California, and not long ago became a director of two **computer-software*** companies—Information Science in West Palm Beach and Forecast Systems in Provo, Utah. In all three endeavors, his aim is to help his fellow man—especially the businessman—develop intuitive decision-making powers to the point where, as he says, "they can control the scientific beast."

Exploring inner space

In preparing for a **lunar** flight, Mitchell explains, "we spent 10 percent of our time studying plans for the mission, and 90 percent of our time learning how to react intuitively to all the 'what if's.'" At Forecast Systems, Mitchell and his **associates*** use the same approach to help **clients*** identify potential problem areas. They interview managers, **foremen***, and workers to uncover their fears about all the things that might go wrong. "With a computer printout of the resulting 'fault tree' in front of him, a CEO can almost smell those failures before they occur," says Mitchell, explaining "failure analysis," a space-age spinoff.

However **methodical**, even scientific, Mitchell and other researchers may be, the explanations of intuition and its powers remain **elusive**. But the businessman like David Mahoney or Ray Kroc who has relied on an occasional hunch to solve an important business problem cares less about analyzing the **phenomenon** than seeing the results. Often, these can be spectacular.

Lunar: having to do with the moon.
Associates: co-workers.
Clients: customers.
Foremen: persons in charge of a group of workers in a factory or on a job.

Methodical: systematic, thorough, careful.
Elusive: hard to find.
Phenomenon: natural event, datum; important occurrence.

1. Business Vocabulary

A.   Next to each sentence write the letter of the word which is *closest in meaning* to the italicized word in that sentence.

A. lower-ranking persons
B. anticipated sales volume
C. estimate of expenditures
D. methodical
E. customers, buyers
F. proof, support
G. incapable, unskillful
H. something bought
I. natural understanding
J. guesses based on feeling
K. hide, cover up
L. depended on

_____ _____ 1. It is difficult to *disguise* the fact that many executives are guided by *hunches*.

_____ 2. *Subordinates* are sometimes surprised by their superiors' decisions.

_____ _____ 3. Even though a proposed new product has good *sales projections*, an executive's *instinct* may tell him to wait on introducing the product.

_____ 4. Edgar Mitchell uses unusual methods for advising his *clients*.

_____ _____ 5. Dave Mahoney *relied on* instinct in everything from picking a wife to picking a company for *acquisition*.

_____ 6. Although *systematic* analysis of a problem is very important, it is not always the only thing considered in decision making.

_____ _____ 7. Certain study, like *cost analysis*, is always done with factual *evidence*, not intuitive feelings.

_____ 8. Only intuition can protect you against the articulate *incompetent* person.

B.   Fill in the blanks with an appropriate form of one of the following words:

foreman   indebtedness
academicians   mutual fund
ingenious   intuitive
fair employment practices   associates
safeguards   computer software

Scientists and _____ are helping business understand its _____ to hunches and _____ knowledge. Howard Stein, chairman of Dreyfus Corp., successfully launched a special _____ made up of companies which complied with environmental _____ and _____. Also, Edgar Mitchell and his _____ use intuitive information along with _____. They interview managers, _____, and workers in the process of creating _____ "fault trees."

2. Structural Review

Verbs plus prepositions

Certain verbs are customarily followed by certain prepositions. It is often impossible to guess which preposition is most commonly used. The following is a list of examples of such verbs taken from the vocabulary exercises in this book. When you learn a verb, you should always make an attempt to learn the prepositions that ordinarily follow it, if any.

To collaborate		with	someone	on	something
To consult		with	someone	on	something
To haggle		with	someone	over	something
To negotiate		with	someone	for	something
To deprive	someone	of	something		
To dispose		of	something		
To protect	{someone / something}	from	{someone / something}		
To profit		from	{someone / something}		
To enroll	someone	in	something		
To invest	something	in	{something / someone}		
To entitle	someone	to	something		
To rely		on	{someone / something}	for	something

Complete the sentences with the proper preposition or prepositions.

1. Is it really safe to rely entirely _____ hunches _____ correct decisions?
2. In fact, too much reliance on hunches may deprive you _____ much helpful input.
3. It is a good idea not to be too hasty; consult _____ your peers about the problem.
4. Collaborate _____ them in determining the primary objectives to be achieved.
5. Give yourself time to consider: haggle _____ prices or spend time negotiating _____ a prospective buyer or seller before playing your hunch.
6. In any case, protect yourself _____ precipitous action.
7. But investing time _____ your decisions is only wise if you have enough of it.
8. Whereas you must not dispose _____ a problem without the greatest possible deliberation, playing a hunch may save you considerable time for other problems.
9. You will profit _____ a delicate balance between data gathering and hunches, and your careful work will entitle you _____ well-deserved recognition.

3. Business Communications

Resumé/data sheet

In searching for employment, the letter of application and the data sheet will be your first contact with a potential employer. The data sheet gives facts about you which the prospective employer will want to know. The purpose of this sheet is to present the most marketable information about you in a format which will appeal to the prospective employer. The data sheet is, then, an important document.

The data sheet should be organized into four sections: personal data, education, professional experience, and references. You do not make reference in the data sheet to the kind of work desired; this is reserved for the letter of application which will be attached to the data sheet (see Chapter Ten).

The personal data section should include only enough information to give the employer an idea of what kind of an individual you are. You might want to include mailing address, phone number, and citizenship.

If you have recently finished school or are still in school, you may want to make the next section, education, the most detailed section. List the schools attended, dates attended, and the degree obtained. You may want to mention two or three courses which are most relevant to the job you are applying for. If you received any honors, grants, awards or if you were a member of a professional society or association, include that information here.

If, however, you have a few years experience working, you should emphasize this more than education. Usually, employers value experience more than education unless it is from a better, well-known school. List your work experience beginning with the most recent and continuing backwards in time. For each job give the dates of employment, the kind of work done, the name of the company, its address, and the name of some person there who can evaluate your work. Employers *do* check these, so be honest.

The last section contains references. Be careful in selecting them. You want to list someone who will speak well of you, and you want someone whose word is respected. Usually three to five are listed. At least one reference should be related to your professional experience, one to your education if you are recently out of school, and a third should be a personal reference.

You may, however, simply say "References will be furnished upon request" if you do not want those people used as references bothered unnecessarily.

Be careful to make the data sheet say what you want the employer to hear. It represents you when you cannot represent yourself in person; do not be satisfied with an inferior data sheet.

Below you will find two examples of data sheets. Study these to see how they differ. After studying the differences, write your own data sheet. When planning, think about who you are sending it to. Make up a hypothetical job and company to whom you want to apply, and write the data sheet specifically for that situation.

DATA SHEET

George C. Coombs
1122 E. Woods Drive
Houston, Texas 10079

Personal Data, May 19– –

Citizenship: USA
Telephone: (413) 444-5739
Military Status: Honorable Discharge

Education

Eastwoods High School, Houston, Texas; graduated, 1969

Junior Classification in Electrical Engineering;
    St. Paul's College, San Diego, California;
    Grade Point Average of 3.4; Degree sought:
B.S. in Electrical Engineering.

Important Courses: Circuits Analysis, Microprocessing, Thermodynamics

Professional Experience

Summer of 1975
    Summer intern for IBM, Los Angeles, California, under
    Mr. Frank Pickle

Summer of 1974
    Summer intern for Acme Business Machines, Austin,
    Texas, under Ms. Jil McCord

Summer of 1973
    Summer intern for IBM, Los Angeles, California, under
    Mr. Frank Pickle

References (by permission)

Mr. Frank Pickle
IBM Corporation
1133 Alemeda Dr.
Los Angeles, CA 84739
(213) 457-5302

Mr. James Black
Professor of Electrical Engineering
St. Paul's College
P.O. Box 687
San Diego, CA 98076
(714) 688-5855

Mr. Ralph Stone
Houston Independent School District
843 Milam St.
Houston, TX 78704
(713) 528-6304

RESUMÉ

PERSONAL DATA   March 13, 19--

Name: Martin J. Flowers
Address: 2231 E. Water St., New Orleans, LA 89765
Telephone: (408) 333-0007

CAREER
OBJECTIVE. . . . . .   To supervise and administer all office functions
                        efficiently and fairly.

FORMAL
EDUCATION. . . . .   BBA degree from Ohio State University, Columbus,
                        OH in May 1973. Major in Office Management.

WORK
EXPERIENCE. . . . .   Assistant Office Manager from June of 1973 to
                        present for TTI Ship Agencies, P. O. Box 987, New
                        Orleans, LA 98364 under Mr. Ralph Reyna.

                        General Office Clerk (part-time) from May of 1971
                        to June of 1973 for the State of Ohio, Columbus,
                        OH 46352 under Ms. Ginny Holstead.

                        File Clerk (part-time) from August 1970 to May of
                        1971 for Strom Shipping Agencies, P. O. Box 549,
                        New Orleans, LA 97423 under Mr. Jack Strom.

INTERESTS. . . . . .   Personal interests include computer retrieval systems
                        and word processing.

REFERENCES. . . .   References can be furnished upon request.

4. Action

Informal class debate

Divide the class into two teams to debate the value of hunches.

Team A: Hunches, or intuitive feelings, should not be given
            serious consideration in managerial decision making.
            Note that precisely how the mind puts things together has
            never been adequately charted; therefore, we cannot
            define the hunch nor can we assess its reliability.

Team B: Hunches should be given serious consideration when
            making managerial decisions. Note that some Gestalt
            psychologists say that sudden ideas come from the
            information processed unconsciously and that in many
            cases such ideas are very reliable and more creative than
            those reached in the normal way.

Allow each team five to seven minutes of group preparation followed by a three-minute presentation (timed by a watch). Allow time for a rebuttal of three minutes by each team.

5. Reaction

Questions for discussion

1. How do you feel about the statement made by Mr. Robert Bernstein that business schools are frightening because they can produce people who are articulate incompetents? He means, of course, that it is possible to graduate from school and be able to use sophisticated business terminology without being personally able to carry out business operations. Do you think this happens? If so, whose fault is it—the school's or the student's?

2. The business which has been established by Edgar Mitchell is unique. What are your impressions of this sort of business? Could it be successful in your country?

3. Scientific management expends a tremendous amount of money studying, measuring, and analyzing business problems in an effort to make the wisest decisions. The article indicates, though, that some executives pay only "lip service" (meaning that they do not take it seriously) to such highly mathematical and scientific data. These executives pay more attention to "gut" feelings and hunches. Do you believe this statement accurately represents the truth of how management makes decisions? If it does represent the truth, even for a few managers, how do you feel about this method of making decisions?

4. Making decisions based on feelings or hunches means that only one person is making the decisions. This reflects the way many decisions are made in the United States. In some other countries, however, decisions are usually made by consensus. Can hunches play a part in decision making in all styles of management?

ANSWER KEY

CHAPTER ONE

Business Vocabulary

A. (p. 7)

1. environmental	7. operations
2. processes	8. mobilized
3. gaseous	9. proposals
4. resources	10. protection
5. prevention	11. efficiency
6. innovation	

B. (p. 7)

multinational	scenarios
annual	services
by-product	managed
refinery sludge	marginal profit
increase	effluents

Structural Review

A. (pp. 8–9)

1. English Clays has been using its china wastes to make prefabricated houses.
2. The Treasury Department has stationed men in the plant to make sure that no alcohol is converted to drinking liquor.
3. Such major companies as Shell and BP are directing their own development by forecasting from scenarios.
4. Hylsa of Mexico is using the sponge iron process to implement direct reduction technology and to prevent massive pollution of its coke furnaces.
5. Companies can avoid costly delay by becoming concerned about environmental impact ahead of time.
6. A company can increase profits by focusing its attention on waste avoidance.
7. At 3M all corporate personnel from the shop floor upward are mobilized to contribute their knowledge and observations.
8. Plants have efficiently lessened pollution by recovering materials for reuse.
9. In Germany more than 200 companies have set themselves up by providing environmental products and services.
10. The corporation is surviving by adapting to its environment.
11. ENKA-Glanzstoff AG is increasing marginal profit by recovering zinc from its rayon plant effluents.
12. By 1976, 3M had decided to attack the problem at its roots by applying its know-how.
13. The company is increasing profits by focusing attention on waste avoidance.
14. Some companies are turning waste to profit by taking a positive view of pollution.
15. A company can grow by investigating new areas in which to develop products and services.
16. The technology of an industry must have a good margin for improving efficiency to economize by means of a no-waste approach.

B. (p. 9)

1. instead of	4. in
2. of	5. of
3. in	6. for

CHAPTER TWO

Business Vocabulary

A. (pp. 17–18)

1. a	6. a	11. a	16. c
2. b	7. c	12. c	17. a
3. b	8. c,b	13. b	18. b
4. a	9. b	14. c	19. c
5. c	10. b	15. a	20. b

B. (pp. 18–19)

1. maker	5. generators
2. director	6. disposers
3. violators	7. treaters
4. transporter	

Structural Review

(p. 20)

1. got, to	7. get, to
2. got, to	8. get, to
3. have	9. make
4. have	10. made
5. get, to	11. had
6. get, to	

Business Communications

(pp. 22–23)

Sample notes:

1. a. In 1980 laws were passed: held waste generators liable for health and environmental risks and required wastes to be cleaned up. Hercules had to help pay for cleaning up wastes dumped before 1980.
2. a. Resource Conservation and Recovery Act (1976) regulates disposal of hazardous wastes.

b. Waste disposal industry is helped by RCRA. They transport, store, and dispose of hazardous wastes.

c. Waste disposal industry will be helped by even tougher laws.

3. a. Since 1960s the trash business has changed from being handlers of ordinary trash into being a modern industry.

b. Congress created new laws because of public opinion which demanded more protection for public health and the environment.

4. a. The RCRA created the regulations.

b. Generators must consult a list of 200 substances which have been classified as dangerous.

c. Once a year, generators, transporters, treaters, storers, and disposers of hazardous wastes must report to the EPA how much waste they handle and how they handled it.

CHAPTER THREE

Business Vocabulary

A. (p. 28)

1. perceive	9. commendation
2. deprive	10. violation
3. protect	11. perception
4. promote	12. intention
5. intend	13. deprivation
6. commend	14. promotion
7. violate	15. protection
8. tempt	16. temptation

Memorandum (p. 29)

violate	intends
promotion	commendation
tempted	promoted
protection	intention
deprived	deprive
violation	

B. (p. 29)

1. actuarial	6. officers
2. liabilities	7. attorney
3. recession	8. labor force
4. subsidiary	9. deadline
5. consultants	10. white collar

C. (p. 30)

at will	labor force
just cause	employee relations
middle management	due process
upward mobility	

Structural Review

(p. 31)

1. Very few age discrimination cases used to be taken to court.

2. Older managers used to be helpless before ADEA.

3. White-collar workers never used to sue their own companies.

4. The number of age bias suits brought by individuals used to be low.

5. Older white-collar workers used to have more faith in their own companies.

6. There used to be less pressure to move older executives out.

7. Corporations used to feel that there was no danger in firing older executives.

Business Communications

(pp. 31–32)

Sample summary:

(1) Age discrimination is common. Businesses prefer younger employees. This keeps costs lower and allows room at the top for advancement. (2) Age bias can be expensive because of the ADEA. Companies are being sued. (3) Lawsuits are jury trials and these favor the employee. Many companies have paid large amounts of money in suits. (4) The EEOC helps employees. (5) The EEOC will be busy because the labor force is getting older. Companies will be wanting to retire their older managers.

CHAPTER FOUR

Business Vocabulary

A. (pp. 40–41)

proliferating	duplication
attract	orientation
negotiation	extension
produce	production
discontinue	supervision
frustrated	

B. (p. 41)

1. b	6. b
2. c	7. c
3. a	8. a
4. c	9. c
5. c	10. a

Structural Review

(p. 43)

mentioned	started
have begun	has grown
have offered	have seen
caught on	have gained, gained
has increased	have profited, profited
have begun	had
initiated	wanted
has been	called
have gained	

Business Communications

(pp. 44–45)

1. c	3. b
2. a	4. c

CHAPTER FIVE

Business Vocabulary

A. (p. 51)
1. nonprofit, negotiable
2. defects, merchandise, haggle
3. bins, values
4. unload, bear
5. price tags, retail prices
6. go for, inventory, depleted
7. secondhand, consignment
8. shrunk, altered
9. garments, lines
10. wardrobe, apparel

B. (p. 51)
1. A shopper who does not give up can frequently find values.
2. Some stores handle only completely unused merchandise, given to them by retailers.
3. One person bought so much clothing that she had to expand her closet to make room for her vast new wardrobe.
4. One store was selling a suit for $85; a similar quality suit would cost $250 retail.
5. There are several small and hard-to-see dangers in buying secondhand clothing.
6. The thrift stores frequently have a policy of taking anything given to them.
7. Men's clothing is usually harder to find.
8. Sizes written on labels can give a false impression and if the wrong size is bought, the mistake is irremediable.
9. When buying furs, it is especially easy to buy one you cannot use or sell.
10. The advantages of used clothing are well known.

Structural Review

(p. 52)

had shopped	had declined
found out	was
bought	had been, were
bought	began
had unloaded	had belonged
found	had been
had been	began

Business Communication

(p. 53)
1. Central Idea: C, Secondary: a, b
2. B, a, c
3. D, b, c
4. A, b, e

CHAPTER SIX

Business Vocabulary

A. (p. 61)

retailing	assemble
market	funds
outlets	confident
expanding	transactions
consumers	merchandise mix
retailer	product returns
warehouses	operating

B. (p. 62)

1. I	6. G
2. C	7. D
3. F	8. J
4. B	9. A
5. E	10. H

Structural Review

(p. 63)

are appearing	will be accelerating
are proliferating	will be entering
are gaining	are demanding
will be expanding	will be launching

CHAPTER SEVEN

Business Vocabulary

A. (p. 70)

assertion	objectionable
motivation	opportunistic
consider	guarantee
presumption	restraint

B. (p. 71)
1. presumption
   presume
2. connotations
   connoted
3. capital
   capitalistic
   capitalism
4. characterization
   characterize

C. (p. 71)

1. laissez-faire	4. private sector
2. free enterprise	5. profit motive
3. assets	

Structural Review

(p. 72)

All underlined verbs *may* be used in the present perfect progressive tense.

Business Communications

(pp. 75–76)

1. Figure 8

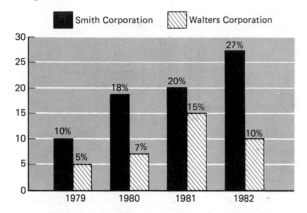

2. Figure 9

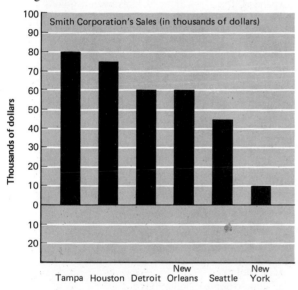

3. Figure 10

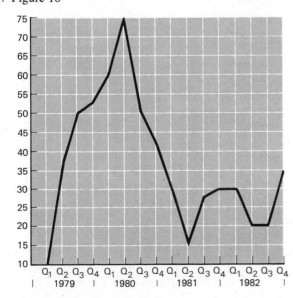

4. Figure 11

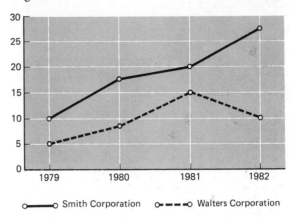

5. Figure 12

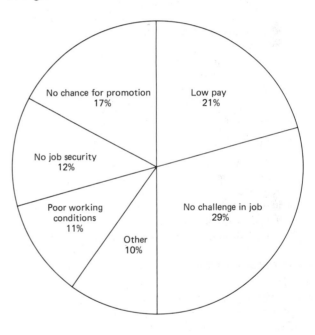

CHAPTER EIGHT

Business Vocabulary

A. (p. 84)

1.	c	6.	b
2.	b	7.	a
3.	c	8.	b
4.	a	9.	a
5.	c		

B. (pp. 84–85)

1.	b	6.	a
2.	a	7.	c
3.	c	8.	c
4.	b	9.	a
5.	c		

Structural Review

(p. 86)

have been teaching	are turning
have been building	are sitting
has been eroding	are importuning
was turning out	will be adopting
were producing	will be offering
was paying	will be initiating
was doing	will be designing
is taking hold	

CHAPTER NINE

Business Vocabulary

A. (p. 95)

1.	N	6.	B	11.	D
2.	G	7.	G	12.	E
3.	I	8.	K	13.	F
4.	H	9.	J	14.	M
5.	L	10	A		

B. (p. 96)

petty cash
demographic
accumulate
pay-as-you-go

C. (p. 96)

breadwinner
entitled
collaborated
aggregate
tangible assets

Structural Review

A. (p. 97)

1.	Passive	4.	Active
2.	Active	5.	Passive
3.	Active	6.	Passive

B. (pp. 97–98)

1.	considered	9.	is estimated, has been estimated
2.	reduced	10.	was (not) established
3.	been reduced	11.	will encourage
4.	achieved	12.	has risen
5.	is financed	13.	has been created
6.	retains	14.	will be required
7.	are induced	15.	will be perceived
8.	has (not) been replaced		

CHAPTER TEN

Business Vocabulary

(p. 107)
1. embarking, ambitious, energy-efficient
2. fixed costs, curtailing, potential
3. revitalize, capacity
4. proponents, excess, eliminated
5. decline, diversification
6. contemplating, exploitation
7. assurance, ventures, regulators
8. intrastate, access
9. imposes, intensified

Structural Review

(p. 108)

1.	looked for	7.	will be investigated
2.	taken	8.	will be generated
3.	expanded	9.	has been acquired
4.	provided	10.	have been won
5.	are shown	11.	has been suggested
6.	has been changed		

CHAPTER ELEVEN

Business Vocabulary

A. (p. 119)

Suggested answers:
1. reconsider
2. asserts
3. expenses
4. stimulate
5. approximate calculations
6. saving
7. produces
8. estimating for the future
9. increasing

B. (p. 119)

1.	recessionary	5.	cash flow
2.	audits	6.	estimates
3.	allocating	7.	forestall
4.	rate of return	8.	growth industry
		9.	pays off

Structural Review

(p. 121)
1. At one point the Mellon study reported that even the most optimistic projections understated conservation's real potential.
2. The energy management director at 3M Co. said that energy-intensive companies had (or *have*) a real cash flow problem.

3. *Business Week* reported that the market for building energy management systems was expected to grow to $1.8 billion by 1990.
4. The interviewee declared that, already, a conservation industry to supply the necessary products was (or possibly *is*) taking shape.
5. The author wrote that many producers would benefit as conservation became (or *becomes*) widespread.
6. He continued that nearly 1,000 "energy stores" had popped up around the country in the last couple of years.
7. Northeast Utilities stated that companies in the surrounding service area could cogenerate as much as 200 Mw.
8. Exxon stated that energy consumption at the turn of the century would be fully 34% less than 1972 predictions.
9. One official from the Energy Department said that there was no way that an American steel company could compete with more efficient Japanese technology.

CHAPTER TWELVE

Business Vocabulary

A. (p. 131)

1. c	5. c
2. c	6. b
3. b	7. a
4. a	

B. (pp. 131–32)

1. preferences	6. dossiers
2. stockholders	7. directorship
3. accountable	8. corporate responsibility
4. pooling	9. perspective
5. chairmen	

Structural review

A. (pp. 132–33)

1. b	4. f
2. a	5. c
3. e	6. d

B. (p. 133)

1. d	5. f
2. e	6. c
3. b	7. a
4. g	

Business Communications

(pp. 135–36)

Sample telex messages:

Problem 1

> FROM: THERMOSTRONG, NEW YORK
> TO: OSIO INDUSTRIES, LONDON
> THANKS FOR CREDITING $3,487 US AS AGREED 5/6/8- IN CONTRACT NO 9327. WILL SEND INSTRUMENTS IMMEDIATELY.
> THERMOSTRONG

Problem 2

> FROM: SACHS INCORPORATED, LOS ANGELES, CA, 2/20/8-
> TO: SACHS INCORPORATED, SINGAPORE
> CC: SACHS INCORPORATED, NEW YORK
> TWO SHIPMENTS CLOTH LATE HERE. PLEASE ADVISE SOONEST ON PROBLEMS.
> BOOTH
> SACHS

Problem 3

> FROM: SACHS INCORPORATED, SINGAPORE, 2/20/8-
> TO: SACHS INCORPORATED, LOS ANGELES, CA
> CC: SACHS INCORPORATED, NEW YORK
> SHIPMENT ONE DEPARTED SINGAPORE 2/8 ONBOARD VIKING. DUE IN LA 3/15. SHIPMENT TWO TO BE SENT AIR WITHIN WEEK ON SINGAPORE AIR. ARRIVE LA 3/27.
> LEONG
> SACHS

CHAPTER THIRTEEN

Business Vocabulary

A. (p. 142)

1. a	7. j
2. f	8. l
3. g	9. d
4. h	10. i
5. b	11. c
6. e	12. k

B. (p. 142)

1. reawakened
2. continuity
3. reduced
4. representatives
5. failures
6. consideration
7. assistance

Structural Review

(p. 143)

1. had considered
2. would have thrown
3. would have continued, had remained
4. would have been, had supported
5. had defined, would have expressed
6. would have continued, had failed
7. had developed, would have had
8. had felt, would have been
9. had spoken, would have questioned

CHAPTER FOURTEEN

Business Vocabulary

A. (p. 156)
peers
advanced degrees
urban
candidate
predecessors
fields of study
mobile
goal oriented
accelerates
succession
executive search organization

B. (p. 157)

1. e	5. c
2. d	6. a
3. b	7. f
4. g	

Structural Review

(p. 158)

1. better	6. less
2. highest	7. clearer
3. most, more	8. most frequent
4. younger	9. more readily
5. largest	10. more than

CHAPTER FIFTEEN

Business Vocabulary

A. (p. 168)

1. K, J	5. L, H
2. A	6. D
3. B, I	7. C, F
4. E	8. G

B. (p. 168)
academicians
indebtedness
intuitive
mutual fund
safeguards
fair employment
practices
associates
computer software
foremen
ingenious

Structural Review

(p. 169)

1. on, for	6. from
2. of	7. in
3. with	8. of
4. with	9. from, to
5. over, with	

INDEX